Organizational Justice during Strategic Change

Organizational Justice during Strategic Change

The Employee's Perspective

MARCOS KOMODROMOS
University of Nicosia, Cyprus

and

DAPHNE HALKIAS
Harvard Medical School, US

Routledge
Taylor & Francis Group

LONDON AND NEW YORK

First published 2015 by Gower Publishing

2 Park Square, Milton Park, Abingdon, Oxfordshire OX14 4RN
52 Vanderbilt Avenue, New York, NY 10017

Routledge is an imprint of the Taylor & Francis Group, an informa business

First issued in paperback 2020

Gower Applied Business Research
Our programme provides leaders, practitioners, scholars and researchers with thought provoking, cutting edge books that combine conceptual insights, interdisciplinary rigour and practical relevance in key areas of business and management.

British Library Cataloguing in Publication Data
A catalogue record for this book is available from the British Library

ISBN: 978-1-4724-5328-0 (hbk)
ISBN: 978-0-367-60608-4 (pbk)

Library of Congress Cataloging-in-Publication Data
Komodromos, Marcos.
 Organizational justice during strategic change : the employee's perspective / by Marcos Komodromos and Daphne Halkias.
    pages cm
Includes bibliographical references and index.
ISBN 978-1-4724-5328-0 (hbk)
1. Organizational justice. 2. Organizational change--Management. I. Halkias, Daphne. II. Title.
HD6971.3.K65 2015
331.01'1--dc23
                                                    2015012434

Contents

About the Authors

Marcos Komodromos, Ph.D. is an Assistant Professor at the University of Nicosia's Department of Communications and is an Accredited Charter Instructor of Public Relations in Cyprus, Greece and Romania. He has worked in the fields of internal communication, corporate communication and crisis management in both Cyprus and Greece. He acts as business consultant for a range of organizations in Cyprus and abroad. Marcos has more than 12 years' experience in the media industry, particularly radio and TV, and has many media projects to his credit. He has published widely on organizational justice, organizational trust, management of change, internal communication and corporate social responsibility.

Daphne Halkias, Ph.D. is a distinguished academic, researcher, published author, and consultant in the areas of family business, coaching and mentoring, entrepreneurship, organizational psychology, education and sustainable entrepreneurship. She is a Fellow at the Institute of Coaching, McLean Hospital at Harvard Medical School; Research Affiliate at the Institute for Social Sciences, Cornell University; Research Associate at the Center for Comparative Immigration Studies, University of California, San Diego; and Senior Research Fellow at The Center for Youth and Family Enterprise, University of Bergamo. Dr. Halkias is CEO of Executive Coaching Consultants and Editor of *International Journal of Teaching and Case Study* and *International Journal of Social Entrepreneurship and Innovation*. She is a Member of the Family Firm Institute and is on the faculty at University of Liverpool, UK and International School of Management in Paris.

PART I
FUNDAMENTAL ELEMENTS

Chapter 1

Promoting Organizational Change in the Workplace: An Ongoing Challenge for Organizational Leaders Today

Organizations may be able to maintain their competitive advantage by managing employees effectively and seeking out techniques that promote trust and facilitate change as well as minimize resistance to the latter. Researchers have endeavored to determine pertinent factors that promote trust during change through the use of the organizational justice framework. The organizational justice framework is the degree of perceived fairness of decision outcomes (distributive justice), decision-making processes (procedural justice), and how employees have been treated by their leaders during organizational processes such as in a period of strategic change.

Organizations need strategic change in order to expand and successfully compete in a dynamic market. However, not all changes are successful. In fact, almost 70 percent of the planned strategic change programs in organizations do not accomplish their desired objectives. Negative employee reactions to organizational strategic imperatives have the potential for highly negative impact, significantly interfering with the intended gains of change. As such, it is essential that organizations implementing change better understand potentially negative reactions by employees to the process in the interests of effectively managing the outcomes.

Managerial efforts for strategic change and restructuring in organizations over the past few years have consistently failed in the absence of support from non-managerial employees and their resistance towards the strategic change itself. Employee dedication, sincerity, and loyalty with regard to the management of change largely determine its success or failure. Employee resistance to strategic change leads to increased absenteeism, employee turnover, lackluster performance, feelings of dissatisfaction, and lower morale—all of which can create feelings of mistrust in employees towards management.

Trust in management is driven mainly by how employees perceive fairness and the management of change within an organization. Organizational justice theory provides a means of conceptualizing employees' perceptions of trust, fairness, and the management of change within their organizations. As such, application of an organizational justice framework—inclusive of distributive, procedural, and interactional justice—can offer greater understanding of how employees' personal and institutional trust are related to perceptions of how fairly they have been treated during a strategic organizational change. Employees will regard organizational change more favorably when, from their viewpoint, it has been fairly handled and elements of fairness in management's decision-making process are easily observed.

Among the many concerns organizations have, an important focus is employee perception of organizational justice given the role it plays in attitudes and behaviors of employees. Researchers have extensively analyzed employees' perceived organizational justice showing that organizational fairness has positive and negative impact on various outcomes. In organizational science research, justice is considered to be more understandable in its relation to organizational justice.

Considerable research on organizational justice has evidenced that fairness perceptions are linked to outcomes that are important both to the employees and their employing organization; these include trust, job satisfaction, cooperative work behaviors, and organizational commitment. More specifically, prior research in the area of organizational justice revealed that its dimensions correlate negatively to turnover intention, but are positively associated with trust, job satisfaction, and commitment to one's organization. Furthermore, knowing how employees perceive organizational justice can help anticipate and manage work-related behavior as well as set a high moral and ethical standard. This in turn works to boost commitment to the organization as well as feelings of trust towards supervisor and the organization as a whole.

Social scientists who have investigated the important role justice plays in organizational management support the view that social institutions need to view organizational justice as a priority virtue. In a seminal quantitative study on organizational justice and the management of change, researchers found that the justice framework is optimal for more fully explaining and gaining a better understanding of employees' feelings of trust and mistrust. Perceptions of justice and trust assessments can be relied on as consistent predictors of the attitudes and behaviors of employees. In the literature on organizational behavior, the organizational justice framework has garnered much attention, first appearing in the early 1970s and more particularly in social science research. Organizational justice brings together the methods employed in making higher management decisions, perceptions regarding their outcomes, and the treatment of impacted employees. As such, organizational justice offers insight into employees' reactions in relation to trust and mistrust, and sheds light on the rationale behind them.

Seminal social psychologists have concluded that trust is psychologically important to organizational life. It follows then that scholars call for more dynamic conceptualizations of workplace phenomena, and focus on perceptions of justice and trust assessments for reliably predicting the attitudes and behaviors of employees. When trustworthiness is operationalized with regard to ability, there is a weaker connection between trustworthiness and justice. The skills, competence, and efficiency of managers do not have significant bearing on whether or not they actually adhere to justice rules.

Fairness is deemed a critical element in any aspect of the change process. The perceptions of an entity's fairness can evolve and change through an ongoing cyclical process in which individuals' judgments of justice events are affected by their existing perceptions concerning the entity involved. Many authors support that the perception of an entity's fairness represents a trait-like and global evaluation that is often informed by a series of judgments of justice events involving that entity that are experienced over time. Organizational justice scholars concluded that in the absence of unexpected events, perceptions people have about the entity are relatively stable and resistant to change.

Organizational justice as a contingency framework can be useful for assessing the effectiveness of a change initiative, helping to lessen possible negative effects accompanying change and thus enhancing the overall success of an organization's change implementation. Recent studies on organizational change management have found that positive workplace characteristics and strategies enhance support for and acceptance of change. More specifically, scholars place an emphasis on the content as well as the quality of communications related to the change initiative, on ensuring that the procedures as well as the outcomes are equitable and fair, and on providing employees with support in their adjustments to the change. Furthermore, considering the increasing frequency with which organizations seek to implement large-scale initiatives of strategic change, it is important that researchers and practitioners understand those strategies and managerial actions that both contribute to effective implementation of organizational change and help ensure its sustainability over the long term.

In the justice literature, a central finding is that employees' justice perceptions, beyond being influenced by the outcomes of organizational decisions, are also impacted by the processes employed to make, communicate, and implement work-related decisions. Recognizing the relevance of organizational justice to organizational change, researchers have used the justice perspective as a base from which to examine employees' reactions to organizational change initiatives. Additional empirical research is needed to explore these relationships further and test them in different settings, for example, in varying social contexts or where change is not seen as being successfully implemented.

Organizational leaders often struggle to establish and sustain a trusting culture in times of constant changes in job roles, corporate globalization, global competition, technological advancement, strategic change, and unethical behavior by corporate leadership. Organizational justice theory provides a means with which to explain and better understand employees' perceptions of trust, fairness, and the management of change within the context of strategic change. Empirical studies over the past three decades have confirmed the link between constructs of organizational justice and certain outcomes valued as important by organizations, and the processes yielding the results. However, prior research illustrates how organizational justice perceptions within the same business unit differ considerably depending upon whether one is a manager or not.

Researching employees' perceptions of trust, fairness, and the management of change using an organizational justice framework can have significant implications for human resources management during a time of strategic change. Seminal studies on trust, fairness, and management of change have largely been conducted with public sector employees, and further research is needed to establish if these outcomes can be replicated in other sectors as well as for different events of organizational change. The specific problem is how an organizational justice framework would address the need raised by scholars of organizational justice (for example, Colquitt and Greenberg, 2003; Mayer, Nishii, Schneider, and Goldstein, 2007) for novel, conceptually derived accounts of non-managerial employee perspectives on organizational justice during periods of organizational change.

Chapter 2
Theoretical and Conceptual Framework

In the past three decades, the management literature has focused much attention on the topics of organizational justice, trust, fairness, and the management of change. Seminal scholars have investigated and extended the work on a number of theoretical and conceptual models on the aforementioned topics. Researchers have also developed theories to explore perceptions of fairness and trust in managing organizational change that may influence employees' evaluations of outcomes.

Kurt Lewin is recognized for creating the most controversial organized approach to change. The *"Three Step Model of Change"* (Lewin, 1958)—unfreezing, change, and refreezing—was an outcome of his earlier seminal contributions to areas such as action research, field force theory, and group dynamics. Although authors such as Bullock and Batten (1985; four-phase model) and Cummings and Huse (1989; eight-phase model) tried to improvise the model, Lewin's concept of change and action research set a foundation for research focused on organizational development, and is, in essence, a planned approach to change employing knowledge from behavioral science.

According to Lewin's unfreezing, change, and refreezing model (1951), change originates from two forces: those internally driven (from a person's own needs) and those imposed or induced by the environment. The unfreezing step involves getting people to accept the impending change. The change step has to do with getting people to accept the new state, while the refreezing step intends to make permanent the new practices and behaviors once the implementation process has been concluded. In order to achieve organizational change and to break a given state of inertia, managers and agents of change should strive to achieve the state of refreezing.

Recently, researchers have come out in support of the idea that perceptions of trust and fairness can influence employees' reactions and attitudes towards a change initiative. Neves and Caetano (2006) and Saunders and Thornhill (2003, 2011) studied the role of supervisory trust, justice perceptions, and commitment in implementing organizational change. Findings in both studies concluded that the social relationship between employees and supervisors during change is a critical factor for successful organizational changes. Neves and Caetano (2006) proposed a model of analysis to extend Lewin's change model by suggesting the addition of a process of informing employees about the proposed change in order to understand it and support it.

Organizational justice theory was originally developed from applied research in organizational management. The taxonomy of organizational justice theories by Greenberg (1987) have received strong empirical support citing trends in the research questions concerning justice and workplace perceptions of fairness. Greenberg (1987) focused on more proactive and more process-oriented conceptualizations of organizational justice, combining two dimensions that are conceptually independent: a reactive–proactive dimension and a process–content dimension. Such an approach helped distinguish theorized interrelationships in the professional environment, mark trends in emerging areas of inquiry regarding research on organizational justice, and hone in on points revealing empirical or theoretical deficiencies.

Continuing in this vein, Greenberg (2009) argued that most studies on organizational justice focus mainly on theoretical issues and essentially only regard implications for practice as a secondary issue. As a result, Greenberg (2009) investigated organizational justice and identified such implications for practice in four theory-based studies in order to better evaluate the impact of interventions aimed at promoting justice. Greenberg's findings of theory-based research added to the existing organizational justice theories, illustrating how efforts to test theory-based applications can offer clearer insight into prevailing theories. Other research efforts support Greenberg's (2009) findings and even earlier contributions in this regard. Examples of such efforts include Bartunek and Rynes (2010) and Behson (2011), who illustrated that theory-based application studies promoting organizational justice can benefit organizations and their employees as well as extend the theories on which they are originally based.

Despite their recognized benefits, several reasons exist for why such investigations, in the form of applied studies, have been rarely conducted. First, managers tend to be unaware of justice-related problems and so are unlikely to collaborate with researchers on the topic. Second, some researchers contend that studies seeking to uncover ways of improving the work environment lack scientific objectivity. Third, academic scholars are in favor of research addressing theoretical issues and avoiding practical applications. Recently, applied studies have confirmed Greenberg's (2009) theorem that the context in which organizational justice is assessed may play a role in identifying which justice factors are relevant to employees. Finally, recent research findings have added to the empirical evidence supporting the dimensionality of organizational justice and suggest that dimensionality of organizational justice is more context-dependent than previously thought.

Organizational trust has until recently received relatively little research attention, with most conceptualizations of trust being focused on at an interpersonal level. The literature on organizational trust, drawn from a wide range of disciplines such as sociology, psychology, and economics, has resulted in many conceptualizations of the trust construct. Seminal organizational scholars extracted common themes from various conceptual definitions of trust and proposed a consensus definition: "Trust is a psychological state comprising the intention to accept vulnerability based on positive expectations of the intentions or behaviors of another" (Rousseau, Sitkin, Burt, and Camerer, 1998: 395). The same study confirmed that interpersonal trust is important for the motivation of workers to self-organize, and that where trust is present it can promote a critical mass of trust-related behaviors, such as cooperation needed to create higher-unit trustworthiness.

In addition, Six's (2007) research on developing a theoretical model for building interpersonal trust within organizations supported Rousseau et al.'s (1998) trust theory, and offered more insight into the dynamics of interpersonal trust-building in the workplace environment. In general, trust-building has to do with the logic of appropriateness, where considerations of trust focus on what managers think is appropriate in a certain situation; in other words, each party should desire a continued relationship. Extending work in this area, other authors found that the ability to demonstrate trust in times of change requires managers to engage their employees.

Social psychologists indicate that organizational justice theory is strongly linked to the construct of organizational trust. Saunders and Thornhill (2003) theorized that any influential factors on employees' perceptions of interpersonal justice are critical for building trust in the organization. Saunders and Thornhill (2004, 2011) investigated further on this issue, and used an organizational justice framework to investigate the relationship between trust and mistrust in an organization. The authors contended that various dimensions of organizational justice (perceptions of distributive, procedural, informational, and interpersonal theories) have varying impacts on trust and mistrust. Their theory extended Folger and Cropanzano's (1998) organizational justice theory, which states that leaders' decisions are influenced by subordinates' perceptions of justice. This theory was elaborated on by examining employees' perceptions that made judgments about the actions of organizational leaders.

Greenberg (1990) recognized the importance of fairness theories and models of social and interpersonal justice as important tools to understand employees' behaviors in the work environment. Folger and Cropanzano (1998) extended procedural justice theory by investigating how managers' decisions can influence subordinates' perceptions of justice in organizational life. The authors theorized that negative fairness perceptions are determined by factors related to procedural, interactional, and distributive justice because of the influence of accountability. More recently, other researchers have developed a variety of justice theories focused on the role of emotions and the perception of fairness in organizations.

Contributing to Folger and Cropanzano's (1998) theory of fairness, Colquitt (2001) established the theoretical dimension of organizational justice, consequently supporting a four-factor structure. More specifically, distributive, procedural, interpersonal, and informational justice were to be regarded as distinct entities that, albeit correlated, have differential effects on a number of outcome variables at both the individual and group levels. Colquitt (2001) posited that if the four types of justice are conceptually distinct and seen to predict different criteria, they should be deemed separate constructs. As a result, fairness theory is considered to be an important element of the trust construct, with perceptions of distrust and unfairness leading to resistance or negative and even destructive employee reactions towards the organization.

Integrating present justice theories with research on social cognition and sense-making, Jones and Skarlicki (2012) put forward a model of organizational justice to illustrate the processes that can influence changes in perceptions of fairness. The model asserted that an individual's perceptions and judgments of an event are guided by their perceptions of the entity involved. This study confirmed Folger and Cropanzano's (1998) theory that procedural and interactional justice serve to moderate the perception of degree of fairness of the outcome of management decisions.

Building upon the research of Greenberg (1987), Bidarian and Jafari (2012) added additional understanding to the theories of perceived justice by employees and their interactions with their managers. The authors suggested that a manager's trustable behavior forms organizational trust, and lack of justice does not establish a climate of trust in the organization. Greenberg's (1990) theory on interactional justice supports that employees' perceptions are more positive when their treatment is characterized by dignity and respect, and when they are provided with desired communication. The theory also supports that the current literature discusses distributive and procedural justice as the two most common forms of organizational justice. However, more recent research has given additional emphasis to interactional justice as a distinct aspect of justice in its own right. Cropanzano, Byrne, Bobocel, and Rupp (2001) argued that interactional justice was more observable for employees and thus helps to overcome perceptions of a lack of distributional and procedural justice. Extending this, other researchers have noted that organizational justice should include interactional justice as a third dimension. This ties in well with implications for engaging employees in the interests of more positive socio-emotional responses and identification with their organization and organizational citizenship behavior and cohesion.

Organizational Justice

The construct of organizational justice as discussed in the literature on organizational behavior first appeared in the early 1970s, and most often in the social science literature. Organizational justice is based on employee perceptions, in any kind of organization, that they are being treated in a fair and just manner by their organization. According to Greenberg, organizational justice began to receive attention in order "to test principles of justice in general social interaction, not organizations in particular" (1990: 400). In industrial and organizational psychology, organizational justice is a critical field of study.

Early research supports that organizational justice theory can provide a means with which to explain and more fully understand employees' feelings of trust and mistrust in organizations, and contends that organizational justice is by its very nature a phenomenon. The behaviors of employees in the workplace towards justice evolved into an area of study following the increasing importance attributed to the concept of justice. Research has examined employees' perceptions of organizational justice, enabling discussion on the explanatory value of organizational justice theory. Employees might experience trust and mistrust in an organizational context, and leadership needs to therefore consider that the work environment can influence feelings of mistrust. Theorists support that justice perceptions in the workplace have proven to be a rich and robust area of research over the last years.

Organizational justice theory remains a combination of social psychological theories and psychological contract paradigms seeking to explain fairness judgments. Organizational justice theorists support that organizational justice is associated with fair treatment of people and is thus a critical determinant in their responses to decisions.

A substantial body of research has investigated the impact of perceptions of justice on outcomes including employee withdrawal behaviors (i.e., absenteeism, turnover), organizational commitment, job satisfaction, counterproductive work behavior (i.e., employee theft), organizational citizenship behavior, and job performance. Meta-analysis studies have found that procedural justice, distributive justice, and variations of interactional justice are strongly linked to many of these outcomes. High levels of organizational justice predict high employee performance, high job satisfaction, low withdrawal, more organizational citizenship behaviors, high organizational commitment, and less counterproductive behavior in the workplace environment.

Scholars have extensively examined key concepts of organizational justice as well as employees' reactions to, and perceptions of, different types of injustice in organizations. Several theories and models have been developed to provide enhanced understanding of employees' perceptions of fairness and trust in managing organizational change that may influence employee evaluations of outcomes. The associations between perceived distributive and procedural justice were broadly examined by a number of early organizational scholars in the workplace environment. Researchers (e.g., Lambert, Hogan, and Griffin, 2007) expanded their research on organizational justice through explorations into the effects of distributive and procedural justice on job satisfaction, job stress, and organizational commitment. Results revealed that both these forms of organizational justice negatively affected job stress and organizational commitment. Furthermore, only procedural justice had a significant impact on job satisfaction.

Research into employees' perceptions of trust, fairness, and the management of change using an organizational justice framework, during a period of strategic change, has constituted an important topic in organizational psychology. Numerous questions remained unanswered in the extant literature and much work is needed to improve knowledge regarding accounts of non-managerial employee perspectives on organizational justice and trust in organizations during strategic change.

The Importance of Qualitative Research in the Justice Literature

Employees are an important part of various organizational decision-making processes, but the question often arises as to whether the resulting decisions affect employees fairly or unfairly. The study of employees' behaviors in response to justice in the workplace garnered interest among researchers when the concept of organizational justice began to take on increasing importance. It is difficult to simulate the complexities and dynamics of justice in the laboratory, and they also cannot be adequately understood using traditional, quantitative methodologies. The justice literature could benefit significantly from qualitative studies because the qualitative process allows for an inductive examination of identified problems, enhancing in this way an understanding of the meaning and complexities of certain situations. Qualitative research brings together different strategies, methods of data collection, and interpretations that help the researcher support diverse perspectives regarding how individuals progress from judgments about the fairness of events (e.g., receiving a lower-than-expected raise) to the fairness of entities within the organization. This kind of research is stimulated by Cropanzano et al.'s (2001) comments on the questions and methodologies associated with the two paradigms.

Following a qualitative research approach, the justice literature can also benefit from the etiology of justice in actual events. Qualitative methodology will allow the researcher to more fully examine in-depth and over an extended period how an organizational justice framework can be used and applied in a variety of organizational settings. Such settings will allow researchers to investigate how judgments made about the justice of events are related to justice judgments about the entities deemed responsible for the events, and also how they contribute to the development of both attitudinal and behavioral responses.

Organizational scholars support that, even a few years later, justice remains an isolated anomaly with relatively weak albeit consistent powers of prediction and explanation. Authors support that although such isolation of the justice literature may at one time have had its advantages; it now seems far too costly to leave out. Qualitative research on justice has many opportunities to impact organizational research and management practices if it is included in mainstream thinking in the organizational sciences.

Researchers must consider that it is better to conceptualize relationships between justice dimensions and major independent variables, like group interactions and structure, organizational structure, motivation, or leadership (Taylor, 2001). Giving significant attention is encouraged to increase the research on models that explore some of the relationships mentioned above by Taylor (2001), and also on an increasing number of mediating variables that involve social exchange relations, for example, leader–member exchanges or psychological contract violations. These kinds of variables are apparent in research on both justice types, as well as in a wider spectrum of organizational behavior studies. Following, scholars are encouraged to clarify and extend their considerations of justice findings and their practical implications so as to better demonstrate their importance for research in other areas of the organizational sciences. Qualitative studies make it possible to conduct rich and in-depth examinations of the organizational context in which knowledge sharing takes place, and researchers can interpret and understand phenomena that may emerge from in-depth interviews.

Alternatively, there is a need for more qualitative research that focuses on specific issues so that researchers can improve the design of qualitative studies in the area of employee perceptions in organizational life. A number of authors support that such research shows that individuals describe their experiences of justice in "hot" and emotionally laden terms. Such findings suggest that individuals do not react in an emotional manner just on the basis of rational judgments formed about their treatment. Rather, their initial experience of feelings of unfairness is characterized by the same physiological arousal and inclinations to act expected of numerous emotional experiences. In recognition of this, the use of designs that are richer and more temporally focused is strongly advocated for examining justice perceptions in a more dynamic context, and in consideration of the affective context they emerge from.

Organizational justice researchers suggest that rigorous qualitative research involving interviews or observational exercises can help highlight the proposed interplay among motivational concerns, affect, and the events encountered in the workplace. Barsky, Kaplan, and Beal (2011) previously also referred to this, proposing that such methods could capture the temporal dynamics of a process more richly and highlight, for example, whether emotional responses to an event could influence the experience of future, related events. On the other hand, interview questions probing individuals' non-work affect, for example, as a result of family issues or commuting, help researchers gain insight into whether and when such incidental affect actually feeds into concerns regarding justice, as could observing a work environment's affective tone or climate.

Subsequently, by using these qualitative methods, researchers can over the course of days, weeks, or even longer easily track individuals and measure their experiences of events as well as relevant justice judgments. Considerable attention has been given to the logic of the theory on affective events, as proposed by Weiss and Cropanzano (1996), as its design allows researchers in the organizational justice literature to differentiate the effects of momentary affect and reactions to events and their perceived justice from the effects of more aggregate justice perceptions on behavior in the work environment.

Chapter 3
Dimensions of Organizational Justice for the Employee

Employee Perceptions of Organizational Justice

Over 30 years of analysis on organizational justice provided the research outcome that a person's perceptions of fairness are associated with the results that are significant both to the employing firm and to the employees. Perceptions of fairness in the workplace can be associated with employees' cooperative work behaviors, organizational commitment, and job satisfaction. Greenberg (1987) points out that organizational justice theory has its focus on fairness perceptions in organizations. The theory seeks to explain and categorize the feelings and views of employees regarding their own treatment as well as that of others in the organization, and it is descriptive in nature.

Organizational justice scholars have shed much light on employees' responses to perceived fairness or lack of fairness in the work environment. A review of the literature on this topic supports that within an organization justice is regarded as a social construct and that an act is deemed as just if most employees perceive it to be so. Scholars suggest that employees' perceptions of organizational justice are likely associated with a variety of other individual factors such as organizational commitment, organizational trust, and organizational change. Other factors have to do with pay satisfaction, self-perceptions, and job satisfaction. Also playing a role in perceptions of organizational justice are withdrawal behaviors and job performance. Finally, justice perceptions by employees will be influenced by organization level—those at higher levels are more likely to have a greater sense of justice in view of their better treatment, greater rewards, and influence.

However, employees at lower levels who are experienced with some improvement in their treatment will inevitably regard this more favorably than higher-level employees who are offered the same improvement. Other studies have shown that justice perceptions by non-managerial employees towards management are influenced by the development of close interpersonal relationships that are based on exchanges perceived as fair. This offers support for the existence of different justice foci and indicates how perceptions of justice may be moderated as well as potentially reinforced, either positively or negatively. Employee justice perceptions can be moderated by events, such as strategic change, across an organization.

A meta-analysis study by Cohen-Charash and Spector (2001) confirmed that perceptions of justice "are, in part, considered to be influenced by outcomes one receives from the organization" (p. 282). In this regard, the researchers identified demographic variables (e.g., age, gender, education, tenure, and salary) as well as personality variables (e.g., self-esteem and negative affectivity). Their findings only partially support the idea that characteristics of change outcomes have a stronger relation to distributive justice perceptions than to procedural justice perceptions. In another study, research indicated that organizational justice perceptions have very little direct effect on work performance, but mostly affect workplace performance as a whole. In addition, organizational justice and relationships between co-workers demonstrate the importance of distributive, procedural, and interactional justice in organizations. On the other hand, some research findings reveal that a perceiver's demographic characteristics play only a minor role in perceptions of justice. With regard to personality variables, research has found a more significant negative relation between negative affectivity and procedural justice and interactional justice than in relation to distributive justice. In addition, scholars present support for a third category of influence for justice perceptions, as applied by Cohen-Charash and Spector (2001), in organizational practices—that is, quality interactions and procedures.

Organizational justice is concerned with how employees view organizational fairness and how this affects their behavior. In addition, other studies support that perceptual cognitions play a role in organizational justice and that this is relative to different frames of reference, comparison entities, or relevant referents. Researchers support that the way in which employees perceive justice in organizations has an effect on their attitudes and behaviors. Furthermore, employees' perceptions of justice in their organizations are considered important for the well-being of employees as well as for effective organizational operations.

Employees perceive an organization to be fair based on how the organization treats its employees. When employees have a positive perception of organizational justice they are more likely to enjoy pay and job satisfaction, and be more committed to the organization. On the other hand, when employees feel that there is a lack of justice then they will begin to have thoughts of leaving the organization, employ negative attitudes, and resist change. Organizational justice theory provides a means with which employees' trust and fairness perceptions can be understood. A perception of a justice entity represents an accumulated assessment about the fairness of a particular source of justice, such as a supervisor. Research studies suggest that organizational justice perceptions are integral for organizations to effectively manage resistance to change, prevent low employee morale and withdrawal behaviors, and avoid against a lack of organizational commitment.

Employees' perceptions of trust, fairness, and the management of change within the context of strategic change can be understood effectively with the help of the organizational justice approach. Organizational justice theory can also be used to point out the success or failure of a strategic change process. Meta-analytic results further support this perspective. Organizational change can be more effective if trusting relationships exist between the organization and the employees. Employees' resistance to change is based on their perceptions of justice and fairness; thus, if employees feel they are being treated fairly they will then be positive to organizational changes.

However, given that perceptions of justice may also change over time, recent research notes the importance of studying further how such change can influence work outcomes. This will logically also have implications for attitudes towards organizational change and therefore calls for ongoing improvements in conditions of fairness as well as attention to other factors such as the changing dynamics of employee–management/supervisory relationships so as to ensure more favorable reactions to impending change. As such, both organizational-level and individual-level variables must be factored in when considering perceptions of justice and potential reactions to change.

Researchers have examined the relationships between supervisors and subordinates, to understand and improve them, and establish organizational justice and trust. Employees' perceptions of trust and fairness determine how change is embraced in an organization. The structure of an organization needs to be such that it can deal with both trust and mistrust. Scholars support that the organizational justice framework will help the prediction and management of work-related behaviors of the employees in an organization and conserve high ethical and moral standards at their workplace. This can result in the improved trust and organizational commitment of the employees towards their organization and supervisor. Since employee perceptions of justice have an effect on organizational outcomes, then understanding organizational justice and employees' perceptions of trust, fairness, and the management of change, using an organizational justice framework, is critical because it may assist organizations to improve their processes and productivity.

Dimensions of Organizational Justice

Organizational management scholars highlight various dimensions believed to make up organizational justice; which dimensions constitute it remains a subject of debate. The earliest social justice theories with regard to organizations highlighted distributive justice and equity theory. Seminal research by Cohen-Charash and Spector (2001) came out in favor of a three-factor structure made up of distributive, procedural, and interactional justice. The authors contend that by separating these three dimensions of organizational justice one can better examine and understand the different impacts of organizational justice on trust and mistrust.

In other research, a four-factor structure was introduced further dividing interactional justice into perceptions of interpersonal and informational justice. Colquitt (2001) emphasized that the four types of justice should be deemed separate constructs if seen to be conceptually distinct and predict different criteria. Other researchers have made efforts to organize and integrate different research efforts with regard to the diversity of organizational justice theories. Researchers linked judgments on justice to individual evaluations associated with the constructs of organizational justice.

Organizational justice researchers emphasized a need for more clearly conceptualizing the constructs of organizational justice. In organizational literature, distributive justice and procedural justice are consistently found to have a strong relation to the work-related attitudes and behaviors of employees, as supported by Greenberg (1990). A fairly recent study noted that during periods of change communicating with and informing employees about the "why," "how," and "what next" offers clarification and compelling justification for the change, as well as providing a greater sense of control over it. Saunders and Thornhill (2003) supported that the organizational justice framework can be used to explain and more fully understand the feelings of trust or mistrust on the part of employees. Viewing these dimensions of organizational justice as distinct and separate makes it possible to explore differential impacts on organizational trust and mistrust.

Recent research highlighted how the dimensions of organizational justice can be used to the benefit of employees and organizations, enhancing desired outcomes such as trust and commitment. The three types of organizational justice—distributive, procedural, and interactional—are negatively associated with employees' turnover intentions and positively related to organizational outcomes and employee behaviors, such as supervisory and management trust, and job satisfaction. Organizational scholars support that employees' organizational justice perceptions are positively related to their workplace attitudes; as a result, this has a positive impact on an organization's overall management as well as the quality of employees' work life. Organizational justice perceptions can be used to predict and help control the behaviors of employees in organizations, and also to maintain high morale and loyalty in the work environment.

DISTRIBUTIVE JUSTICE

Scholarly research on organizational justice supports that distributive justice integrates fairness perceptions regarding organizational outcomes. This type of justice develops when outcomes are in agreement with implied norms for allocation, such as equality or equity. In times of change, an organization needs to be especially attentive to employees' perceptions of fairness of proposed organizational outcomes so that the organizational change can be successful; when employees are considering whether an outcome is fair or appropriate, they are in effect making a distributive justice decision. Employees notice the relative distribution of salaries and benefits in the organizational context, merit pay, and budgetary funds, and this is considered to be an essential element of the distributive justice perspective.

There is substantial research in support of the critical role that distributive justice has in important individual and organizational outcomes. Given that feelings of trust are affected by comparisons of the relative treatment and outcomes of others, distributive justice is closely related to trust. When employees feel that there is distributive justice, they are more likely to feel more trusting towards management. Relevant to distributive justice, research studies have shown that those managers deemed more competent and efficient in the workplace are regarded as less fair in their allocations of outcomes. The authors supported that this result was surprising, "as one would expect high levels of ability to translate into a more accurate perception of employee inputs" (Colquitt and Rodell, 2011: 1200).

Scholars support that distributive justice focuses on outcomes, mainly in relation to cognitive, affective, and behavioral reactions to a particular result. Among the three dimensions of organizational justice, distributive justice is the strongest construct, being associated with trust in management, job satisfaction, and lower turnover intentions. It has also been linked to satisfaction regarding outcomes as well as commitment to the organization. In addition, recent research supports that distributive and procedural justices can help an organization's leadership and management to improve on job satisfaction and organizational commitment of employees, as well as lessen turnover intentions.

PROCEDURAL JUSTICE

This concept is based on people's evaluations of fairness with regard to compensation or any other managerial judgment. Procedural justice research emphasizes that decision control is considered an important contributor to perceptions of justice in the workplace. This type of justice focuses on the processes employed to make such decisions. As early as 1998, Folger and Cropanzano supported that since procedural justice emphasizes the perceived fairness of how the amount of punishment or reward is determined, the way in which outcomes are determined possibly holds greater weight than the final outcome. In line with this view, in a seminal study by Saunders and Thornhill (2003), procedural justice is seen as the perceived fairness of processes employed in the distribution of responsibilities, compensation, and rewards. Additionally, a relationship exists between procedural justice and trust, with fairness perceptions of treatment (interactional justice) being very important in enabling trust in the organizational environment. This same study also found that the way in which managers treat employees can lead to increased perceptions of organizational support and enhance the trustworthiness of a manager.

Organizational behavior scholars indicated that through its impact on attitudes, procedural justice may affect the performance of employees. In a comprehensive review, Greenberg (1987) highlighted that procedural justice contains evidence of process theories, both reactive and proactive, which concern procedural justice or fairness used to determine an allocation's final outcome. Reactive process theories describe people's reactions with regard to dispute-resolution procedures, and deal with reactions to injustice from proactive theories that attempt to prescribe means directed towards attaining justice. Proactive theories exemplify allocation procedures.

Research has also shown that employees' behaviors and actions can be influenced by procedural justice. Recently, various researchers have suggested that employees' perceptions of procedural justice refer to their beliefs regarding how decisions on actions are made. Further, seminal studies showed that perceptions of procedural justice could promote employees' acceptance of change outcomes even when these are seen as unfavorable. Researchers make distinctions between the latter (social accounts) in individuals' work, and give little attention to interpersonal sensitivity.

Scholars suggested that specific dimensions of justice combine together and shape overall perceptions of justice in the work environment. These relationships have been explored in relatively few studies in the literature on organizational justice. Distributive justice, interactional justice, and procedural justice are shown to be the strongest predictors of overall perceptions of justice. Interactional justice was found to be the weakest predictor of overall perceptions of justice, and that procedural justice and interactional justice could only explain significant differences in overall perceptions of justice. To enable further clarification of the relationships between these constructs, scholars suggest that the multifoci model of justice developed by Cropanzano et al. (2001) highlights a need to take into account who or what is being evaluated.

Procedural justice research has been conducted on various topics, such as organizational commitment, trust, and mistrust. Scholars note that employees' perceptions of procedural justice are linked to their satisfaction with supervisors and commitment to the organization. Employees will exhibit greater loyalty to and trust in the organization and will be willing to work for their organization's best interests if they perceive that a decision-making process is fair.

INTERACTIONAL JUSTICE

Also known as interpersonal and informational justice, interactional justice focuses on leadership and management. It refers to how adequate the information that is used to explain how decisions are made is and how thoroughly accounts of these decisions are provided. Interactional justice focuses on the quality of interpersonal treatment an employee receives during the implementation of organizational procedures. According to Folger and Cropanzano (1998), this type of justice refers to the quality of interpersonal treatment an individual receives, both before and after a decision has been made.

Interactional justice is more concerned with the feedback and concerns of employees in organizations, with knowledge and information being provided in cases where employees express related concerns, as well as the explanations and information given to employees by management that provide detail on fairness procedures and outcome distribution. Interpersonal justice refers to the extent to which management treats employees with politeness, dignity, and respect. Informational justice focuses on interactional justice, which has been linked with job satisfaction, satisfaction of outcomes, withdrawal behavior, organizational citizenship, commitment to an organization, and performance.

Evidence shows that there is a relationship between interactional justice and employee perceptions regarding how they are treated by their managers. Organizational scholars note that since the treatment of employees in an organizational setting is closely related to trust, and employees' trust is an important ingredient for successful organizational change, management needs to seriously take into account interactional justice in times of strategic change.

Chapter 4

Organizational Justice and Trust

Organizational Trust

A substantial body of the empirical literature on organizational trust focuses on fields related to organizational behavior, organizational science, anthropology, psychology, and sociology. Recent research highlights the importance of organizational trust as a factor that can promote successful business practices, within and between organizations. Trust reduces conflict, enables interactional behavior, and can decrease transaction costs at work. The trust construct is a key element promoting effective communication as well as team work between co-workers, and between employees and managers. Within the trust literature, seminal authors have observed that trust significantly drives down uncertainty in organizations and improves cooperation among employees and between employees and managers, or any parties that need to work together in the organizational environment. The three-dimensional organizational trust model is based on the assumptions that an employee (or group of employees):

1. makes good-faith efforts to behave in line with implicit and explicit commitment;

2. is honest in any negotiations preceding such commitments; and

3. does not excessively take advantage of others even when an opportunity to do so presents itself.

Organizational trust is a constructive and vital ingredient promoting organizational effectiveness, and it is seen as a competitive advantage for organizations.

In the literature on trust, the definition of trust has been the subject of much debate. Seminal authors developed their own model of organizational trust to define trust in the workplace. These authors defined trust as being open to a trustee's actions based on expectations that the latter will follow through on a particular action, notwithstanding any control or monitoring mechanisms. The researchers highlighted that various concepts belonging to the confident, positive expectations approach can be used to predict trust as they defined it. Other authors have defined trust as "a psychological state comprising the intention to accept vulnerability based upon positive expectations of the intentions or behavior of another" (Rousseau et al., 1998: 395). When individuals are interactively involved in trust-building, action and trust can mutually reinforce each other. As Rousseau et al. state, "trust is not a behavior, but it's a condition that can cause or result from action" (1998: 396).

Organizational trust is essential for successful cooperation and effectiveness in the workplace. Organizational trust scholars conducted a meta-analysis study that recounted the evolution of workplace trust studies. According to their study, and building on Saunders and Thornhill's (2004) work supporting this, organizational trust is an important factor in order to reduce the complexity in organizational relationships. Most theoretical writings on organizational trust argue that behaviors which build trust are linked to strategic business outcomes, and that trustworthy management does not have to deal with the high cost of turnovers as their employees do not leave the organization and drive business results.

Trust is at the core of all interpersonal relationships—it holds people together and offers individuals a sense of security. Seminal authors sought to better understand the role of trust, defined as a willingness to be vulnerable in accordance with the positive expectations of another's intentions or behaviors, and how trust in management can improve performance in an organization. Other authors support that when employees feel that management trusts them this enhances their performance in the organization and their productivity. Organizational justice and trust have received great attention in the past several years on the strength of evidence that justice perceptions and assessments of trust are consistent predictors of attitudes and behaviors on the part of the employee.

Social psychologists support that organizational trust has to do with an employee's confidence and support in their employer, and that this is a prelude for successful collective actions in organizations. This approach also corroborates Saunders and Thornhill (2004), who suggested that trust reduces uncertainty, in addition to complexity, as unfavorable expectations are removed and favorable expectations are seen as certain. Other studies have suggested that organizational trust is linked to a variety of behavioral and performance outcomes, including fairness, change, job satisfaction, communication, and commitment to the organization. Organizational trust incorporates the belief that leadership or management will be straightforward and meet their commitments.

During strategic change in organizations, perceptions of outcomes may influence employee trust. Trust is a crucial element in organizational change initiatives, and can be considered as an important factor for successful cooperation and effectiveness in organizations. Employees who feel trust can focus on positive aspects when talking about their reactions to organizational change, since these employees are more enthusiastic and promote positive working relationships with their colleagues and their line managers. Organizational trust can be seen as a base for having confidence in and feeling secure about the intentions and actions on the part of supervisors, managers, and leadership.

The results of Saunders' (2011) exploration of the nature of trust in relation to employees' treatment during strategic change strengthen the case for paying careful attention to factors influencing personal trust and impacting institutional trust during periods of change. Employees who only felt trust to some extent considered only personal or institutional aspects of trust when justifying their feelings. More specifically, employees' overall feelings of trust are likely to be more significant when they feel trusting at both an organizational and personal level.

Organizational trust may be a prerequisite to establish organizational effectiveness. Trustable behavior between supervisors and employees can positively affect organizational results and have an influence on employees' attitudes toward their organizations, such as in promoting the organization's functions, performance, and efficiency, thus boosting productivity. In addition, when managers promote fair and transparent decision making to their subordinate employees, it becomes easier to build organizational trust between managers and subordinates as well as drive employee productivity. When managers offer honest justifications and explanations to their subordinates, the results are continued trust in their supervisors and confidence in their trustworthiness.

Furthermore, organizational trust is associated with individual human behavior and effective group and organizational functioning. Organizational behavior scholars have argued that a significant relationship exists between the concepts of organizational justice and trust. Investigating the relationship between these two concepts, research by Bidarian and Jafari (2012) showed that there is a strong relationship between the two, and that employees are more willing to promote their functions and performance and be more efficient in order to increase organizational productivity. Other researchers highlight the importance of how trust perceptions can mediate procedural justice and turnover intentions.

Ethical organizations take care of their employees and work to build their trust in the firm through positive communication efforts. Organizational trust scholars developed and tested a model to examine employees' perceptions of trust in management and how these perceptions affect the sense of responsibility, as well as performance in sales. As such, trust affects overall organizational performance. Saekoo (2011) elaborates on this, noting that organizational trust is key for successful workplace relationships and can motivate people to commit to their organizations.

THEORIES OF ORGANIZATIONAL TRUST

Organizational trust researchers defined trust in different ways in order to include intra- and inter-organizational meanings of trust. Seminal scholars developed a trust construct in order to define organizational trust. These authors support that others can trust a person because they know it is in that person's self-interest to be committed to them, and this is where trust can be seen as the basis for commitment and positive relationships in the workplace. Interpersonal and contextual organizational variables both influence trust, and an important predictor of employees' trust is the fair treatment that they receive from leadership and management in the organizations.

The willingness to be vulnerable is considered an important factor in defining trust. Furthermore, risk-taking and interdependence have been discussed as core factors in the emergence of trust; as interdependence increases, changes take place in the nature of the risk and organizational trust. Thus, risk creates an opportunity to develop organizational trust.

Scholars have argued that relational trust between the trustor and trustee develops from repeated interactions over an extended time period, and that most conceptualizations of trust place an emphasis on the interpersonal level. These authors' organizational trust model supports that dependability and reliability perceived by employees through past interactions is likely to increase positive expectations with regard to the trustee's intentions. The importance of such an approach was also noted in earlier research on the topic of trust. Consequently, trust can also be described on the basis of its multiple causal roles, including trust as a cause, moderator, or outcome, and that which is impacted by any kind of change in the organization.

Individual behaviors are seen as a part of trust-building, helping individuals to learn about the intentions of others on the basis of observation and interpretation, and to make judgments about trustworthiness and act upon these judgments. Other researchers developed theories in order to better understand the importance that trust in a supervisor has in organizational change initiatives; they argue that first one must examine how trust is built. The fairness with which employees are treated by leadership constitutes a predictor of organizational trust, and was found to be positively related with all three justice dimensions—distributive justice, procedural justice, and interactional justice. Organizational justice and trust theories emphasize their importance in achieving desired performance outcomes and finding ways to trigger discretionary behavior in employees and management.

DIMENSIONS OF ORGANIZATIONAL TRUST

The topic of organizational trust increased interest in marketing and organizational studies. Recent research studies on organizational trust highlight the importance of trust in business environments because it reinforces effective communication and work relationships between managers and employees, especially in times of change. Scholars argue that it is possible to distinguish between different types of trust, and that leadership must understand how different dimensions of trust play a role in different types of trust. Therefore, it is necessary to understand what expectations co-workers, managers, or employees have of each other in the workplace.

Organizational trust is not just critically important for any kind of organization; it is the essential element of organizational success. Trust has been conceptualized and operationalized in different ways and across a number of levels, as from subordinate levels to leadership levels. For example, several studies in organizational behavior examined interpersonal trust, which is the trust that exists between individuals in organizations. Interpersonal trust is linked with different perspectives considering both social context (organizational policies) and individual behavior.

Scholars focusing on the concept of organizational trust have argued that organizational trust is not a simple and unified concept. More recently, both academicians and practitioners supported that trust is a key success for individual and group behaviors in the workplace. Although current theory and definitions of organizational trust have until now focused on the consequences of placing one's trust in action and the risks that accompany this, scholars support further focus on what is appropriate in a given situation, "to act appropriately" (Six, 2007: 305); in other words, in a normative frame.

Research has shown that a willingness to trust is positive related to perceptions of another's trustworthiness. Extending this, Fulmer and Gelfand (2012) found that on the part of the trustee, ability, benevolence, and integrity — the three dimensions of trustworthiness—contribute to trust in interpersonal referents. Perceptions of ability are positively correlated with trust in interpersonal referents, where benevolence is indicated as a key predictor of interpersonal trust. Relative to ability and benevolence, perceptions of integrity are positively correlated with trust in interpersonal referents.

A key predictor of trust in the workplace is the degree of fairness with which organizations treat their employees. Fairness theory provides a more complex discussion of the mechanisms through which perceptions of justice might be changed. Different authors examined the interaction of justice and trust in the workplace between managers and subordinates. Recognizing that a non-trusting workplace environment can result from loss of productivity and negative organizational impact, research has shown that justice and trust are critical for organizational relationships and for understanding processes in organizational communication. Trust is regarded as a constructive and critical ingredient necessary for promoting organizational effectiveness and that it can influence employees' attitudes towards the organization and promote organizational productivity.

Organizational Justice and Trust

Despite the emphasis on trust in the relevant research literature, scholars still do not know enough about what makes employees trust organizations. Studies examining organizational justice have found that fairness perceptions are linked to trust in management and organizations. Employees' perceptions of organizational trustworthiness partially mediate the relationships of managerial practices and procedural justice with trust. Justice has been found to be a stronger predictor of trust in organizations, based on the interactions of organizational justice and managerial practices. Furthermore, the dispositional propensity of employees to trust organizational leadership can be explained by their perceptions of organizational integrity and of how the three types of justices are linked to organizational procedures.

Different authors define trust differently. Organizational trust refers to the expectations of an individual (or group of individuals) that another individual's (or representative group's) word, promise, verbal, or written statement may be relied upon. As such, it follows that trust is the belief or confidence in a person or organization's integrity, fairness, and reliability. Organizational trust scholars believe that organizational trust offers many important benefits for organizations and their employees.

Organizational justice research has suggested that perceptions of justice can be formed with regard to a number of 'targets' within the organizational environment. For example, an employee receiving fair treatment from a supervisor but not from co-workers will have different justice perceptions about each party. Empirical work using a multifoci perspective of justice has found support for this differentiation of perceptions of justice and outcomes on the basis of different organizational foci.

Following this line, Frazier, Johnson, Gavin, Gooty, and Snow (2010) examined the effects of justice perceptions on perceptions of trustworthiness and interpersonal trust in leadership. Results indicate that there are differential effects of procedural, interpersonal, and informational justices on trust, and that trust in a proximal referent enhances an employee's ability to focus on work-related tasks, but that trust in a distal referent does not have the same such effect. Hausknecht, Sturman, and Roberson (2011) and Lilly, Virick, and Hadani (2010) posited that perceptions of different types of justice, which tend to reflect judgments of justice events, do indeed change over time.

Organizational trust is a significant element for effective day-to-day functioning of the organization. Further, when fairness is believed to be present in an organization, it is possible for trust to be built up. Organizational trust is an important factor for reducing complexity in organizational relationships, and promotes justice and fairness in the workplace environment. The absence of trust in the strategic change process can result in cynicism, which can definitely be detrimental to the effectiveness of organizational change.

Scholarly research on organizational trust in the workplace suggests that subordinates' trust in their supervisor is an important predictor for positive organizational outcomes, such as higher job satisfaction and other desirable workplace attitudes (e.g., organizational commitment) and behaviors. Supervisors must consistently engage in fair and competent behaviors so that subordinates trust them. Employees' perceptions of fairness reduce uncertainty in relation to dilemmas, such as whom to trust, in the work environment and what kind of organizational outcomes will be provided over the long term.

Other studies have linked organizational justice and trust to behaviors that organizations regard as important. Researchers have also examined how interactions between multiple foci of trust and organizational justice affect employees' perceptions of their enlarged roles. Findings revealed organizational trust is a critical factor for employees' construals of perceptions of fairness and their professional roles. Trust-enhancing interventions in the workplace need to be combined with organizational changes in relation to fairness.

Focus on organizational justice in the workplace can influence organizational trust and support. Overall justice is the proximal driver of outcomes in an organization, with individuals responding to their general justice experiences and thus influencing those outcomes. The process of organizational justice and excellent employee relationships encourage a positive attitude to create trust in organizations, resulting in risk reduction and operating costs. Perceptions of organizational justice are an important antecedent of organizational trust, job satisfaction, and commitment to the organization.

Procedural justice is found to have a positive relationship with organizational trust and this is considered to be a key variable in strengthening employee–organization relationships needed to encourage organizational strategies. In times of strategic change, it is important for employees to trust their management and that the change process is perceived as a fair one. Multifoci research on perceptions of justice and trust in organizations has established that employees can form justice and trust perceptions in a number of authority referents in the workplace. Employees who feel they can trust leadership are better able to focus on activities that produce value, which in turn leads to improved organizational outcomes.

A large body of research in social psychology and philosophy supports the idea that justice is the first critical factor for assessing the quality of relationships between organizations and their employees. Social scientists have suggested that organizations view justice as the "first virtue of social institutions" (Greenberg, 1990; van den Bos, 2001) as it affects employees' attitudes in relation to managerial trust. When individuals enjoy a mutually trusting relationship, action and trust will reinforce each other. Building trust on an interpersonal level is a two-way, interactive process wherein each party contributes to mutual trust and positive behavior.

Subordinates perceive management's behaviors through various communication exchanges in the workplace. When subordinates trust their managers in the workplace, procedures that have been designed to ensure fair treatment can be promoted successfully. Organizational justice is important in order for employees to develop trust in their organization's leaders and fairness perceptions in decision-making procedures can increase employee trust in management. Past research revealed that higher levels of perceived interactional justice (made up of informational and interpersonal justice) are related to higher levels of trust in the supervisor. Justice and its administration is a basic and intrinsic human need, and its existence has resulted in a better development of human societies throughout history.

Seminal scholars in the area of organizational justice have investigated the consequences of just and unjust treatment by work organizations. This literature has been summarized in three different meta-analytic reviews. Although these quantitative reviews differ in some specifics, they all underscore the propitious effects of workplace justice. In one of these studies, reviewing 25 years of research on organizational justice, scholars found that all three justice dimensions (distributive, procedural, and interactional) could be used to predict trust. In another seminal study, the statistical correlation between organizational justice perceptions and trust were found to be as high as 60. Findings by Tremblay, Cloutier, Simard, Chenevert, and Vandenberghe (2010), also lend support to the research results. Organizational justice allows employees to maintain trust in an organization even when things do not go as they would have liked, such as in the case of an unexpected or unpopular strategic change. The negative effects of such a change process are less severe if an organization is able to maintain procedural and interactional justice. In addition, the authors concluded that organizational justice is firmly linked to trust, as well as commitment, citizenship behavior, customer satisfaction, and conflict resolution.

Organizational Justice and Psychological Contract Violation

Organizational justice studies support that employees' behaviors and attitudes in the workplace environment are significantly impacted by their perceptions of fairness. Organizational justice and trust are widely heralded as imperative for achieving desired performance outcomes and triggering discretionary behavior in employees. Adding to such considerations, other research notes that psychological contract also has an important influence on employee behaviors and attitudes.

Organizational justice beliefs are based on the psychological contract, which is effectively a negotiated "fair" exchange between two parties (Rousseau, 1995). The author defined the psychological contract as "individual beliefs, shaped by the organization, regarding terms of an exchange agreement between individuals and their organization" (Rousseau, 1995: 9). Seminal organizational scholars regarded the psychological contract as an individual's understanding of various reciprocal obligations expected during exchanges with their employer. To better understand how fairness expectations develop, particularly in relation to the workplace, organizational justice researchers have also relied on literature on the psychological contract. In addition, organizational justice theory has enabled many studies of the link between organizational change and psychological contracts. Findings support that the treatment of employees during times of change impacts the nature of individuals' psychological contracts and, as such, it follows that a breach or violation of psychological contract will negatively influence the contributions of employees to their organization. To illustrate, when an organization breaks its promise in relation to remuneration or job description, employees are likely to react in a negative manner on the basis of the perceived violation of the psychological contract. In the case of an unwarranted job transfer, and demotion in particular, the theory on psychological contracts offers that such a move can affect employees' physical and mental health depending on how the change in status is perceived—that is, their experience of the violation of psychological contract if the change is seen as the organization's non-fulfillment of promises made.

Given the significance of the psychological contract within the organizational membership framework, considerations of this variable can be linked with earlier observations that engaged employees will have more positive socio-emotional responses and identification with their organization as well as organizational citizenship behaviors and cohesion. Within the literature, some researchers have considered a transactional or relational orientation to differentiate the nature of employees' beliefs regarding an exchange agreement. For Rousseau (1995), trust in one's employer, high identification with the organization, personal integration in the workplace, high affective commitment, long-term commitment, and contribution make up an employee's relational psychological contract. In relation to reductions in pay or an unwarranted job transfer, it follows that such factors are thrown into a state of imbalance and that employees may seek to restore balance through adverse behaviors, such as theft and/or withdrawal. Withdrawal, the author notes, can be related to both relational and transactional breach, with employees seeking to compensate through other distributive means (e.g., using work hours for activities not pertinent to the job).

Fair treatment of employees is seen to demonstrate their value to the organization and is also an important predictor for their sense of belonging. Organizations need to be more cognizant of the effects of organizational change on psychological contract, and how its breach or violation might lead to negative employee behaviors and attitudes. When employees believe there has been a breach of psychological contract, this is likely to lead to dissonant cognitions with regard to their group membership and, invariably, a negative impact on the employee–organization relationship. This has implications with regard to reduced job satisfaction, reduced citizenship behavior, increased deviant work behaviors, turnover intentions, and even incivility in the workplace. Such responses to perceived unfair treatment or change outcomes have been found to have a significant negative impact on identification with the organization and thus dramatic consequences for organizational survival. This is especially pronounced in a period when financial rewards are not readily available for use as a motivational tool. In addition, and relevant to turnover intentions, findings from various studies on job transfer, as reviewed in recent research by Paille and Dufour (2012), point to a negative relationship between psychological contract violation and thoughts of moving on from either a specific job post or the professional area of activities in general. It is thus important for managers to be able to determine whether a reduction in pay or an unwarranted job transfer may be perceived as a breach or violation of psychological contract and result in dissatisfaction to such a degree prompting affected employees to initiate a job search.

Psychological contract breach is a subjective experience and refers to an individual's perception that the other party has not adequately fulfilled its obligations in relation to the psychological contract. This can happen even when there has not been an actual breach. Psychological contract breach experiences can create doubt and uncertainty regarding the fairness of procedures used by organizations to meet promised obligations. Undoubtedly, the justice climate affects how employees see the organization as well as their desire to remain a part of it, and is thus a key factor in employee–organization relationships. Other authors have also emphasized the role of organizational justice as an important foundation for the strength of employee–organization relational ties.

The importance of these findings is evidenced in research revealing that when employees view organizational justice procedures as fair and consistently applied, they will be more forgiving of minor discrepancies or view psychological contract breach as a situational occurrence instead of a permanent condition. As such, consistent and fair treatment, engendering trust, and a high justice climate work to mitigate the negative effects of change outcomes that are considered unfavorable. Also, it is important for managers to realize that organizational change may cause employees to re-interpret their psychological contracts, with implications for future commitment and contribution to their organization.

The literature and findings on the interplay of organizational justice, trust, and fairness with psychological contract breach or violation supports Hausknecht et al.'s (2011) contention that attention to factors such as the changing dynamics of employee–management/supervisory relationships as well as improving conditions of fairness over time work towards ensuring more favorable attitudes about and reactions to impending organizational change.

Organizational Fairness

FAIRNESS THEORY APPLIED TO ORGANIZATIONAL LIFE

Organizational psychologists support that within fairness theory social injustice occurs when one person is able to hold another accountable for a situation where their well-being (psychological or material, or both) has come under threat. Fairness in organizations is important because it affects behaviors and results in the workplace, and can foster effective functioning of organizations. Seminal scholars, such as Cohen-Charash and Spector (2001), contend that organizational practices, organizational outcomes, and the characteristics of the perceiver influence employees' perceptions of justice. Perceived justice has been examined by various researchers, and was associated with important and positive organizational variables, such as job satisfaction, job performance, citizenship behaviors, and commitment to an organization.

Different fairness models reflect a fundamental tenant of managing uncertainty, and help employees in making judgments about justice, which are inherently linked with their need to manage uncertainty in the workplace. Organizational members face uncertainty in their everyday life, which affects their justice judgments and whether or not they can trust their managers. Justice scholars suggest that to manage uncertainty in the workplace, individuals try to anticipate how fairly they will be treated in the future. Fairness is considered an important factor in organizational commitment; employees treated in a just manner are more committed.

Fairness theory has received special attention in the management literature and been put forward as a means of integrating much of the relevant justice research. In this approach, studies incorporate counterfactual thinking and accountability as key roles. Early actions by supervisors or managers can have greatest significant impact on judgments related to fairness. When the organizational environment, internally or externally, is undergoing strategic changes, uncertainty is likely to be high and fairness judgments are most likely to be reevaluated. In this context, a manager's actions promoting fair treatment are more likely to be incorporated into the general fairness impression of employees in the workplace than would be the case in more stable times.

Meta-analytic studies examined the impact of fairness in the workplace in times of strategic change, with results revealing that the impact of fairness was stronger in different countries and cultures, and fairness was shown to be more important when large strategic changes were taking place in the organization. Considering fairness as an important trust element, perceptions of fairness can form key elements of individuals' perceptions of trust. Perceptions of distrust and unfairness can lead to resistance and negative behaviors directed at organizations and management during change.

The exploration of how justice evaluations are made in the workplace provides a framework for organizations on how to guide future behaviors. Seminal scholars have made important contributions to organizational justice research and consider the outcomes people receive in the workplace—typically material or economic in nature—when forming justice judgments. Fairness theory does not reflect on the impact of procedures on fairness outcomes, and offers little in the way of outlining determinants of responses to unfair treatment from leadership towards subordinates in the workplace.

RECENT RESEARCH ON FAIRNESS IN THE ORGANIZATION

Scholarly research on organizational fairness has become a central topic in the management sciences, having been the subject of a number of reviewed articles. Organizational justice scholars conceptualized the importance of individuals' emotional reactions to fair treatment in organizational allocations and exchanges, concluding that such reactions have consequences at both perceptual and behavioral levels. Research on fairness in the workplace notes that employees, before engaging in meaningful behavior, usually evaluate actions on the part of organizational representatives as well as the resulting outcomes. Seminal authors support that employees form judgments about fair and unfair treatment by comparing their situations regarding treatment and outcomes with those of others. In addition, other research has shown that individuals recognize and react to discrepancies in justice treatment in relation to others.

Fairness in organizations is of particular importance because it actually affects behaviors and results in the workplace, fostering effective functioning of organizations. Recent research focused on how fairness in promotion affects perceptions of procedural justice and job satisfaction. In this regard, selection instruments were shown to be considered fairer than other promotion systems in organizations, such as decisions made by supervisors. Perceptions of justice can be influenced by organizational practices, the organizational outcomes an individual receives, and the characteristics of the perceiver. Consequently, other studies suggest that employees' perceptions of justice are significant in the development of other organizational factors, including organizational commitment and job satisfaction. Employees who perceive their workplace as a just and fair one are more likely to enjoy job satisfaction and less likely to leave as they have a higher sense of commitment to their job.

Given that employees place importance on fair procedures and fair outcomes, when they feel procedures and outcomes are not fair they are likely to be more dissatisfied; as such, management has to ensure that the workplace implements systems and procedures that their employees perceive as being fair. Recent studies confirmed that workplace fairness is defined and operationalized in accordance with whether employees in lower levels feel their organizations' procedures (e.g., performance evaluation process) are fair or not. However, other studies point to a strong relationship between organizational justice and work effectiveness when the workplace environment is considered as fair on the part of the employees. As such, these results suggest that factoring in justice (with regard to employee satisfaction and productivity) in the workplace is warranted.

Current literature supports that employees' perceptions of fairness in the workplace are considered more dynamic when employees receive information and experience justice events throughout their employment tenure. In one study covering three measurement periods, researchers found that within-person variance accounted for 24 percent and 29 percent of the overall variance in organizational and supervisory justice, respectively. In another study, researchers proposed a model of organizational justice that integrates current justice theories with research in sense-making and social cognition to describe the processes through which perceptions of fairness within the workplace change. Employees come to expect fairness or unfairness from higher-level organizational representatives; it is on the basis of such expectations that they manage uncertainty and interpret the justice or injustice of events.

ORGANIZATIONAL JUSTICE AND FAIRNESS

Organizational justice focuses mainly on fairness perceptions in the workplace as well as other factors, such as employee behavior towards organizational commitment, trust, and job performance. The behavior and attitude of employees towards their work and the organization are significantly impacted by their perceptions of fairness, as pointed out by various organizational justice studies.

Bakhshi, Kumar, and Rani (2009) refer to Adams' social exchange theory used to evaluate fairness. Researchers note that employees usually pay special attention to the fairness of organizational outcomes. Adams' theory advocated for the determination of fairness through equity, and conceptualized fairness by stating that employees determine whether they have been treated fairly or not, through comparing their salaries with those of their colleagues who perform similar tasks.

Some authors argue that employees perceive resource allocation as fair only when the decisions are favorable to the person making the judgment. Research showed that the procedures used in making decisions could influence employees' perception of justice and fairness. When employees experience inequality, they develop a desire to prove their ability by increasing their output. Scholars support that employees usually justify their desire to quit by finding evidence of unfair distribution of rewards.

Organizational justice and fairness have received increasing attention from scholars in mainstream literature. Given that these terms are often used interchangeably, many authors consider the concepts of justice and fairness to be closely related. On the other hand, some authors support that a key trust element is the expectation of one individual that another will treat them justly or fairly, especially during times of strategic change. The literature on change also notes that perceptions of unfairness constitute an important source of resistance to strategic change in organizations.

Recent research does, however, suggest that organizational justice and perceptions of fairness can be formed in relation to a number of targets within the workplace. For example, an employee may have different justice perceptions about supervisors and co-workers depending on how fairly each group treats him or her. In line with the multifoci perspective, differential treatment by different sources contributes to the formation of different justice perceptions about each source. Based on observations of change-related interactions, procedures, and outcomes, people often judge fairness heuristically. According to fairness heuristic theory, when an organizational relationship is in a state of change, experiences regarding fairness constitute particularly potent factors in shaping attitudes and behaviors. Employees build their judgments of organizations on elements of fairness that can be observed (e.g., distributive, procedural, and interactional), and justice scholars have identified all three organizational justice constructs as moderators of employees' perceptions of fairness related to organizational change.

Chapter 5
The Management of Change in Organizations

Strategic Change

The need for organizations to safeguard their present competitive positions or to enhance them is a guiding force behind the change implementation process. In today's turbulent economic environment, all organizations are currently undergoing some type of change. These periods of adaptive change are often characterized by radical changes. Strategic change represents a radical change, consciously introduced by top managers, that alters key organizational activities or structures in a way that surpasses incremental changes to already existing processes. Various scholars have argued that if the decisions made by an organization and the actions of its managers in relation to a strategic change are seen as unjust or unfair, employees affected by these will experience feelings of anger and resentment.

A substantial literature review suggests that strategic change in organizations involves ongoing initiatives that are introduced from the higher to lower levels of an organization, and that it has a significant impact on the depth of the change effort. Change in organizations can no longer be approached as an irregular event but rather as a continuous activity that affects both organizational and individual outcomes. Scholars have argued that ongoing changes call on employees to modify work routines as well as social practices (e.g., relations with co-workers and managers). In order to cope with the daily challenge of pressured adaptation to new job requirements and circumstances, employees often experience difficulties and tensions in upholding their usual levels of performance. Such changes can test the quality of trust in relationships between managers and employees during the change process.

The strategic management approach is based on the assumption that top management has complete authority to comprehensively change the direction of an organization and bring about significant changes so as to benefit from the active atmosphere. The second approach, on the other hand, is directed at bringing about changes for improving the productivity of individuals as well as the organization as a whole. This is a more inclusive approach of organizational change. Therefore, the relationship between strategic change and garnering the support of employees for the same is essential for successfully promoting transformational organizational change.

Research has shown that employees' behaviors in support of the proposed change are positively influenced by their commitment to change; however, organizations often have difficulty in successfully motivating the needed levels of employee commitment to change. The management of strategic change can invariably create uncertainty and where such change involves people, this often proves problematic. Where change is perceived as threatening, it is likely to meet with resistance, and thus requires careful implementation to overcome fears. Employees' feelings of threat are ameliorated when trusting relationships exist throughout the organization. Human resource practices can therefore be crucial in the management of change, whether it is incremental, or continuous through the creation and maintenance of trust. Therefore, making trust an integral aspect of employee–organization relationships can facilitate change sustainability.

ORGANIZATIONAL JUSTICE AND STRATEGIC CHANGE

One of the more remarkable aspects of organizational change research is the reporting of a low success rate for strategic organizational change. Evidence points to the failure of some 70 percent of all change initiatives. A major reason for this is a dissonance between the value system of the change intervention and whether employees affected by the change evaluate it as just. Organizational justice is one of the key moderators affecting commitment to change, cooperation, values–congruence fit, and behavior supporting change in the context of organizational strategic change.

Researchers describe organizational justice as the views harbored by employees on justness and honesty in the treatment meted out to them by the organization. Early justice research has its base in the social psychological and legal disciplines. Organizational justice as a construct has over time evolved into a four-factor conceptualization, made up of distributive justice, procedural justice, interactional justice, and informational justice.

Justness of the process utilized in the assessment and fairness in the outcomes obtained in the organization are also part of organizational justice. Distributive justice is generally the first accepted type of justice, and it refers to justness in the results obtained. Other research suggests that distributive justice is the source with which to understand the views of employees regarding remunerations, promotions, and other such outcomes. The higher the fairness in the outcomes, the greater the effort exerted by employees towards accomplishing the desired results.

Promotions, performance appraisals, incentives, and the sharing of various opportunities within the organization are some of the procedures considered by employees when determining fairness in procedural justice. If procedural justice is at a high level, employees have greater trust and participation in strategic decisions, factors that enhance the acceptance of change processes.

Interpersonal justice, on the other hand, is more about the way in which employees are treated. The focus of this justice dimension is on how authority figures, or those with decision-making power, interact with those potentially affected by the decision or change being implemented—regardless of the procedures used in the process or its outcomes. Compared to procedural justice, interactional justice is believed to mainly impact outcomes at an individual level, while procedural justice impacts outcomes at an organizational level. Interpersonal justice impacts the trust that employees have in management and also plays a part in the way they are treated as people during the strategic change process.

One recent study described informational justice as "the amount of fairness in the information, which is used in the decision-making process" (Greenberg and Baron, 2008: 48). Employees tend to believe the decisions even though they may be unfavorable, provided the reasons for the same are communicated appropriately. Thus, informational justice has a significant role in determining the trust factor, especially during the process of implementing strategic change within an organization.

Organizational scholars support that organizations undertake strategic changes to keep up with the demands and rapid pace of environmental changes. Organizational change may take place continuously or incrementally. Despite the many theories, implementation strategies, and approaches to the management of change proposed, successful organizational change remains elusive.

The Management of Change in Organizations

Management's role in the management of executing change is a critical issue for successful outcomes of strategic initiatives. Strategies for the management of change include communication to share information with employees while addressing their concerns to the management, and provide additional training when needed. Recent research investigated the role of middle management in implementing strategic change in an effort to highlight principles that can improve successful strategic implementation. It is clear that the management of day-to-day functions of middle management is of great importance, and that through their behaviors and thoughts managers can contribute to strategy.

Scholars have argued that organizational change is necessary for organizations to survive and prosper. Researchers support that in cases where change is perceived as threatening, employee resistance may increase, and organizations need management to implement successfully the change procedure. Seminal scholars emphasized the important role that human resource practices can play in the management of change, in order to maintain trust.

Researchers support that organizational members' perceptions of trust and fairness are critical in times of change. Recent research examined franchisees' trust and fairness perceptions during a strategic change process. Research results revealed that perceptions of distributive, procedural, and interactional fairness help to increase franchisees' trust perceptions. In addition, franchisees' perceptions of unfairness and distrust lead to resistance or negative and even destructive reactions to the strategic change process.

Globalization and economic instability have prompted an increase in organizational changes related to downsizing and restructuring as a means of improving financial performance and competitiveness. In organizational change research, there have been studies focusing on how to prevent, reduce, or overcome resistance to change, and how to prepare the organization for managing strategic change. Researchers agree that managers' inability to fully understand what is necessarily needed in order to guide their organizations through successful change, can be a reason for failure. Proper planning and management of change can reduce the likelihood of failure and promote change effectiveness, and increased employee morale.

Trust, Fairness, and the Management of Change Using an Organizational Justice Framework

The study of perceptions of workplace justice often focuses on how employees feel about the implementation of organizational methods and proceedings by leadership and management, and their place in such processes. Saunders and Thornhill (2004) suggested that management must focus on perceived fairness since organizational justice is considered to have a positive impact on employee trust, where expectations are based on perceived motives and treatment. Employees' perceptions of trust, fairness, and the management of change, within the context of strategic change, can be understood effectively with the use of the organizational justice framework.

Seminal studies examined the role of supervisory trust, employees' justice perceptions, and organizational commitment in the context of organizational change using an organizational justice framework. Research results concluded that the role of communication and the social relationship between employees and supervisors during organizational change is an important factor for successful change. If employees are informed about the proposed change in organizations they can understand it better and support it.

Building upon the research of Saunders and Thornhill (2003), Saunders (2011) added additional understanding to employees' perceived feelings of trust and their relationship with their perceptions of treatment during organizational change. In a case study of a public sector organization implementing strategic change, Saunders (2011) used the organizational justice framework to explore employee trust reactions, from a sample of 27 employees. Results revealed that employees who felt trust and had positive feelings of treatment within the organizational context were willing to get involved in the change process, and appeared to adopt positive working relationships with their colleagues and their line managers. Other studies also support this perspective and where trusting relationships exist throughout the organization, employees may respond with positive feelings for change.

Another seminal study further explored employees' perceptions of justice and the importance of these for building trust in an organization. Researchers noted that employees' trust and mistrust feelings emphasize how important it is for leadership and management to be sensitive to employees' needs during organizational change so as to enable and maintain trusting relationships. Employees' trust in management enables positive organizational performance.

Authors have also emphasized that employees' perceptions of trust and the role of trust in a supervisor play an important role in implementing organizational changes. The role of communication with employees is an important factor in enabling trust during change, influencing the willingness to become vulnerable. However, as Hausknecht et al. (2011) has pointed out, achieving this necessitates continued improvements in and assessments of perceived conditions of fairness.

The management of change is often linked to strategic leadership whereby leaders influence the organization in its efforts to achieve an aim or goal. Further research supports that when employees perceive unfair justice in the workplace they show poor work attitudes and limited commitment towards organizational objectives. Using an organizational justice framework, researchers explored and explained the nature of employees' reactions to strategic change. The organizational justice framework is useful for analyzing and understanding employees' reactions with regard to trust, fairness, and the management of change in times of organizational change.

Organizational justice studies support that employees' behaviors and attitudes in the workplace environment are significantly impacted by their perceptions of fairness. Organizational justice is thus considered a basic predictor of trust in organizations. Using an organizational justice framework can support scholars in their efforts to conceptualize employees' perceptions of trust, fairness, and the management of change in organizations and offer a greater understanding of the relationship between each of these variables and organizational justice.

PART II
CASE STUDIES

Chapter 6
Research Methodology

Organizational leaders often struggle to establish and sustain a trusting culture in times of constant changes in job roles, corporate globalization, global competition, technological advancement, strategic change, and unethical behavior by corporate leadership. Organizational justice theory provides a means with which to explain and better understand employees' perceptions of trust, fairness, and the management of change within the context of strategic change. Empirical studies over the past three decades have confirmed the link between constructs of organizational justice and certain outcomes valued as important by organizations, and the processes yielding the results. However, prior research illustrates how organizational justice perceptions within the same business unit differ considerably depending upon whether one is a manager or not.

Researching employees' perceptions of trust, fairness, and the management of change using an organizational justice framework can have significant implications for human resources management during a time of strategic change. Quantitative seminal studies on trust, fairness, and management of change have largely been conducted with public sector employees, and further research is needed to establish if these outcomes can be replicated in other sectors as well as for different events of organizational change. Qualitative studies have yet to be conducted on how an organizational justice framework would address the need raised by scholars of organizational justice (for example, Colquitt and Greenberg, 2003; Mayer et al., 2007) for novel, conceptually derived accounts of non-managerial employee perspectives on organizational justice during periods of organizational change.

The purpose of this qualitative study was to examine how an organizational justice framework can be used to explore employees' perceptions of trust, fairness, and the management of change during a period of strategic change in a privately-owned media organization based in Cyprus. A multiple-case study research design was used to satisfy the goal of this exploratory research and data was collected through multiple sources, including in-depth individual interviews, and subject matter expert (SME) review and reflection of the data collected. The researcher conducted eight in-depth, face-to-face interviews with employees from a media organization located in Cyprus. Data were also collected through the maintenance of field notes, and SME of and reflections on the subject matter and data. Additionally, SME examination on the subject matter provided formative evaluation of the interview guide/instrument and SME reflection on the data collected provided an unbiased and objective view in the analysis phase. Triangulation of data sources was conducted to establish credibility of the researcher's reflections on the phenomena under study. The aim of this study was to increase knowledge regarding how an organizational justice framework could address the need raised by justice scholars (e.g., Colquitt and Greenberg, 2003; Mayer et al., 2007) for new, conceptually derived accounts of non-managerial employees' perspectives on organizational justice during periods of organizational change. A multiple-case study design was used in this study to focus on eight participants from a media organization in Cyprus that is undergoing a strategic change.

Semi-structured interview questions were used in this study to extract participants' in-depth perceptions on trust, fairness, and the management of change in a media organization undergoing strategic change where participants can provide their in-depth perceptions. The central research question of this study was focused on the following:

Q1   How can an organizational justice framework be used to explore employees' perceptions of trust, fairness, and the management of change within the context of strategic change?

Sub-questions were as follows:

Q2   How can an organizational justice framework be used to explore employees' perceptions of trust within the context of strategic change?

Q3   How can an organizational justice framework be used to explore employees' perceptions of fairness within the context of strategic change?

Q4   How can an organizational justice framework be used to explore employees' perceptions of the management of change within the context of strategic change?

Other interview questions were used to focus on participants' perceptions of trust, fairness, and the management of change using an organizational justice framework in times of strategic organizational changes.

Research Method and Design

The purpose of the research design selected for this study was to interpret and understand the phenomena that could emerge from in-depth interviews, and this is the reason why a qualitative research methodology was selected. Qualitative research involves an understanding of different experiences, perspectives, and meanings that individuals or groups attribute to a human or social problem. Qualitative research is characterized as a situated activity that locates the observer in the environment being studied, and consists of a set of interpretive and material practices that make that environment visible. Qualitative researchers examine phenomena in the environments where they occur naturally and attempt to interpret or make sense of these phenomena in relation to the meanings individuals attach to them. As such, qualitative research can be regarded as involving an interpretive, naturalistic approach to the world. For the purpose of this study the researcher employed qualitative methodology in order to elicit appropriate qualitative information as to effective inclusion instruction from the viewpoints of non-managerial employees.

This was one of the reasons that exploratory research could be a viable option for research on trust during strategic change. A common tool utilized in exploratory research, and the one that was used for this research, is multiple-case study design. The case study research design has proved effective in various and varied disciplines such as education, social work, political science, and nursing. A multiple-case study design provided this researcher with information such as how an organizational justice framework can be used to explore and understand employees' perceptions of trust, employees' perceptions of fairness, and employees' perceptions of the management of change during a period of strategic change in a media organization. In the initial process of defining the research questions, key assumptions were made and, consequently, data analysis was directed by those questions.

The research design of this study addressed the purpose of the study and helps interpret and understand the phenomena that could emerge from in-depth interviews, and this was the rationale for selecting a qualitative research methodology. This methodology provides tools for researchers to study complex phenomena within their contexts. Eight employees from a media organization in Cyprus constituted the units of analysis for this study, with the goal being to replicate findings across cases. It is important that the cases are carefully chosen given that comparisons were drawn in order for the researcher to predict similar results across cases or, based on theory, predict contrasting results.

Qualitative research strives to evolve an understanding of the experiences, views on, and meanings that people or groups of people attach to a personal or social problem. When conducting qualitative research, some of the objectives that researchers have include diagnoses of situations, screening of alternatives, and the discovery of new ideas. To satisfy the goal of this exploratory, multiple-case study design, the researcher collected data from a varied range of sources.

The qualitative approach involves examining, from the specific to the general, research problems so as to gain a clearer understanding of the meaning and complexities of certain situations. Using different strategies, data collection methods, and interpretations qualitative inquiry is guided towards the support of philosophical assumptions and varied points of view. Data collection, for example, could include the digital recording of interview sessions and researchers' handwritten field notes. In addition, qualitative research design makes it possible to develop different interpretations relevant to the topic under study — these can prove useful for contributing to unanswered questions, emerging themes, and recommendations for future research.

The qualitative case study method seeks to grant a better understanding of an issue or event and its complexity, thus lending itself to the answering of 'How' or 'Why' questions related to events that a researcher has little or no control over. Most often applied in relation to complex and highly contextualized phenomena that present a set of variables unsuitable for control, a qualitative multiple-case study research design is well suited to investigations seeking to understand how people view and interact with their environment. Moreover, this particular research design produced contextual data that enabled an in-depth look at contemporary events or issues, such as strategic change in an organization that had no boundaries. Furthermore, the multiple-case study approach allows researchers to more directly compare similarities and differences in implementation practices in the various settings or contexts under study. This design also enabled investigators to arrive at more generalized conclusions based on the totality of their specific observations.

Using the case study approach can prove valuable for rising above the particular area of research so as to determine elements that are practical and theoretical, empirically valid, and able to be tested. In addition, this particular research strategy can be quite useful in illustrating and determining areas for future research. Researchers indicate that with the help of the case study approach it is possible to comprehend the areas and processes that are dynamic, experiential, complicated, and difficult to understand. Thus, case studies may help in understanding employees' perceptions of trust, fairness, and the management of change within the context of strategic change using an organizational justice framework.

This research study was based on approaches suggested by Yin (2009). This multiple-case study utilized research protocols for research design, preparedness, data collection and analysis, and sharing of results. Initial steps call for developing theory and selecting cases to support the processes of design and data collection. The logic behind this approach was that each case comprised an entire study, the convergent findings of which were ideally replicated by other individual cases. Other steps suggested by Yin (2009) involved an analysis of replication logic and why individual cases produced different results. Replication logic needs to be applied in multiple-case studies, and their sample selection, so findings can be interpreted for the entire set of samples and also to decide if findings support the wider pattern of conclusions.

The selection of multiple cases in this study was based on replication logic as select criterion used to identify prospective participants for each case. Selected participants for this study were non-managerial employees in a media organization in Cyprus. Management-level employees were not included in the group. During study design, cases were chosen on the basis of expected results and theoretical framework. In this study, theoretical replication was supported on expectations that the disposition of each case produced varied or contrasting results.

Replication logic was demonstrated in this study by using select criterion to identify and solicit participants for this case study. Validation was implied in case studies by using replication logic to apply the same exact research questions and approach. In accordance with the approach of Yin (2009), this study employed replication logic by posing the same interview questions to each participant. In case studies, questions of "how" and "why" are used to generate an expanded source of information for complex patterns of results. To gain an in-depth understanding of participants' perceptions, perspectives, and experiences with the phenomena under study, semi-structured interview questions were used as the sole method of data collection in this multiple-case study. By using semi-structured questions during the interview process, insights emerged from understanding of concepts, meanings, emergent phenomena, and linkages that participants articulated from collective responses.

A multiple-case study focused on eight participants from a privately-owned media organization was conducted, and a cross-case synthesis of research findings was carried out. Each participant selected for this study is currently active in sales, or carrying out responsibilities as a technician or cameraman. Multiple-case studies tend to be more difficult to implement than the single-case structure, but resultant data can provide greater confidence in the researcher's findings. Descriptive case studies are most commonly used in both structures and support rich and revealing insights into the experiential world of a particular case.

The use of replication logic in case studies also allows for developing a rich, theoretical framework. Similar to cross-experimental designs, various authors have stated that theoretical frameworks offer a base for generalization to new cases. By evaluating each case as a separate investigation in this study, generalizations were supported by replication logic. For multiple-case studies, the use of replication logic has been likened to multiple experiments. Theories or hypotheses about the selected cases, essential for case study analysis and design, can be used to derive replication logic. For each case, the researcher applies further logic to develop consistent protocols for the collection of data. For the purpose of this study, the researcher developed semi-structured interview questions and the same questions were posed to each of the eight participants. Replication logic was utilized for data collection consistently for each case. The final steps in this study involved the analysis of data and writing up of research results.

Case studies can also follow either the deductive approach, wherein the theory which is already present is utilized for analyzing a specific aspect, or the inductive method, wherein, as a result of the theory on the topic being incomplete, case studies are conducted to broaden, develop, and create theory. The present research was more deductive in nature as it utilized existing theories to better understand, through the framework of organizational justice, employees' perceptions of fairness, trust, and the management of change within the context of strategic change.

Some researchers have noted that one of the biggest issues facing qualitative researchers is that of how many cases should be a part of the multiple-case study approach (e.g., Nonthaleerak and Hendry, 2008). Studies have indicated that the greater the number of sources, the greater the confidence emerging from the study findings. The present study used multiple cases, an approach which enhanced its relevance. The appropriateness of using multiple sources of data collection for the case study approach is substantiated by Yin (2009), according to whom the benefits of a case study data collection approach may be enhanced if various sources of data are used. Data collection for this qualitative multiple-case study was based on participants' responses to the semi-structured interview questions. Participant interviews were digitally recorded and transcribed. Handwritten field notes were made to further document participants' key responses.

This data was subjective and open to interpretation by the researcher, so therefore was classified as qualitative data. Yin (2009) highlighted various sources that can be used for data collection, including interviews, documentation, archival records, direct observations, participant observation, and physical artifacts. The author also recommended using multiple sources of evidence during data collection to explore the range of historical, attitudinal, and behavioral issues in a case study. This combination of approaches provides for greater strength and validity of the research outcome.

Digitally recorded interview transcriptions for each case were created in Microsoft® Excel documents using NVivo software (Version 9) and coded to record frequently occurring words, themes, and meanings. The use of replication logic in this study was allowed for an analytic generalization in order to compare previously developed theory with empirical results. This embedded multiple-case study was special because it was focused on contemporary events and issues centered on compelling theoretical frameworks. Results from each case study were compared to Greenberg's (1987) organizational justice theory, Rousseau et al.'s (1998) organizational trust theory, and Folger and Cropanzano's (1998) theory of fairness.

Having followed the approach of Yin (2009, 2012), replication logic is needed to show external validity, and that reliability is to be determined by the ability of the case study to be replicated in the future with similar findings. To this end, sufficient documentation is needed to ensure that the researcher can replicate the same procedures conducted in the initial study. To help ensure reliability, the author ascertained that researchers used protocols and databases to capture relevant case study information. The researcher replicated this study because contact information of the media organization and participants, as well as interview procedures, and relevant information about the study were securely stored in hard copy and electronic files. Other researchers could replicate this study by performing Internet searches to identify media organizations in Cyprus that are undergoing strategic changes. These interview questions can be used to conduct future case studies regarding media organizations in Cyprus that are undergoing strategic changes with select participants (non-managerial employees) who work in such organizations. Researchers can review research design and data collection procedures described in this study to align methodology with future studies.

Various researchers have pointed out that the case study approach may be helpful for comprehending a specific aspect in its natural environment, which might otherwise be difficult to understand. Other researchers have also highlighted the fact that the case study methodology is quite suitable when contextual factors have significant relevance to the phenomenon being researched, and for which the laboratory or controlled surroundings would not yield a true outcome. This is specifically true of the present study where employees' perceptions during the strategic change process were likely to differ with regard to aspects of trust, fairness, and the management of change in the specific context of a media organization in Cyprus.

Population

The population for the current study was consisted of non-managerial employees of large-sized organizations in Cyprus, a population of approximately 30,364 employees working in large-sized organizations located in Cyprus. Large-sized organizations are defined as businesses that employ more than 249 employees. The media industry is comprised of companies responsible for transfer of information, concepts, and ideas to both general and specific audiences through television, radio, newspapers, Internet, and magazines. The sample of eight non-managerial employees chosen for this study was appropriate since it represents approximately 20 percent of the non-managerial employee population in the organization under study.

Sample

SAMPLING CRITERIA

The current study employed purposeful selection of participants who were interviewed to generate responses. Researchers' sampling strategies should align with the purpose of their studies, resources available, questions being asked, and constraints being faced. Researchers support that the logic and power of purposeful sampling lie in supporting the intent of this research and in selecting information-rich participants where the researcher can learn a great deal about the issue of central importance to the purpose of the inquiry. In this study, eight individuals currently working for a privately-owned media organization in Cyprus voluntarily participated in this study. The total number for the eight in-depth face-to-face interviews was an acceptable number for this qualitative multiple-case study. Replication logic was demonstrated in this study by using select criterion to identify and solicit individual participants for this case study. Study participants had at least three years of work experience in the media organization, currently active in sales, or carrying out responsibilities as technicians or cameramen. In addition, 100 percent of the participants were Cypriot in ethnicity, Caucasian, and the age range was from 22 to 55 years old. Methodologists support that no more than 10 participants may be used to reach thematic saturation for a qualitative study, and that long interviews with up to 10 people are sufficient for a qualitative study. Saturation is defined as the point after which new data collection will not shed further light or greater understanding on the topic being investigated.

SAMPLING STRATEGY

Data was collected through purposive sampling through individual, in-depth, semi-structured interviews. The strategy for selecting participants for a purposeful convenience employs a small group of homogeneous participants that provides an information-rich sample. This sampling strategy requires the researcher to be immersed in the research field, to establish continuing, trusting relationships with participants to address the research problem in depth. As a result, a small number of cases—less than 20—helped the researcher to associate closer with the participants, and enhanced the validity of a detailed, in-depth inquiry in a naturalistic setting.

A pilot study was conducted as a basis for confirming the applicability and dependability of the research questions and data collection techniques of the research. Three participants were selected through purposive and snowball sampling. These participants had knowledge of the research purpose and their results were not part of the full study.

For the full study, the number of participants was initially set at eight and could grow depending on the data saturation point. During data collection, data saturation is achieved when any new information obtained offers few or no changes to the coding or analysis of data already amassed and also does not give further insight into the topic being studied. As such, a consideration of data saturation plays a significant role when defining a qualitative study's sample size. In addition, it is important for researchers to keep in mind that more data will not necessarily translate to more or better information for analysis and interpretation. This approach was taken in this study by focusing on the desired outcome: a small sample of carefully chosen study subjects would favor in-depth understanding of a phenomenon, while a large sample would support an investigation by giving it breadth.

SAMPLE SELECTION

Essential criteria for selecting participants included participants who have experienced the phenomenon under study, and were interested to participate with their consent to the interview and allow publication of the collected data. The criteria for selection included non-managerial employees who had at least three years of work experience in the media organization, currently active in sales, or carrying out responsibilities as technicians or cameramen, and had good and ample information on the issues under study. Study participants fell within the full, permitted range of age groups, and it was assumed they offered a range of different views and opinions on the topics being investigated.

Permission to conduct the study at the media organization was requested and granted by the General Director of the media organization under study. Following, prospective participants were contacted either in person or by telephone with an invitation to take part in the study. Volunteers who accepted the invitation were interviewed either in person or through telephone contact in order to gather basic information and ensure that they are of legal age as well as eligible to take part in the study. Once eight non-managerial employees were identified as study participants and responded positively to a letter of invitation by email, they were supplied with a Letter of Consent form. All employees who agreed to participate in the study and signed the Letter of Consent were contacted by the researcher to set up a personal interview.

All eight participants were referred to by number rather than by name for the purpose of this study, to maintain their anonymity and confidentiality. Participants were not asked to provide confidential or proprietary information about the media organization they work for. Replication logic was demonstrated by asking each participant the same interview questions. To avoid discrimination, prospective participants were not screened on factors such as age, gender, race, religion, or cultural background. Individuals who agreed to participate in this study were informed about the methods that were used in this study, and participants were identified by numerical classification.

All eight participants were informed that they would receive electronic copies of the research results as was noted from the beginning of their interview.

Materials/Instruments

Data for the study was collected through individual, in-depth, semi-structured interviews. One purpose of a case study is to shed light on decisions that the participants have made. Questions should focus on meaning, and the instrumentation itself is crucial to the success of the study. The interview guide for the present study was developed to determine trends, experiences, and themes of study participants in relation to the phenomena under study. A semi-structured interview format was used in this study as it lends itself to adaptability. This feature is particularly important for case studies, in that each participant's experiences will be unique and therefore questions may need to be adapted. Structured interviews, such as those used for quantitative studies, are not appropriate due to the lack of depth of information collected. Open-ended questions, as commonly used in a semi-structured interview, are better suited for qualitative studies in order to identify themes and subtle nuances in the participants' answers.

Interview questions were aligned with topics covered in the literature review section of this qualitative, multiple-case study. Each study participant received a letter of introduction relevant to the particular research and call for participation as well as an informed consent form that was signed. The researcher used open-ended, semi-structured interviews to collect responses. Interviews were "focused" in nature; that is, short, not exceeding an hour. The interview protocol consisted of:

a)   the opening (welcome and indication of objectives);

b)   the body (interview questions); and

c)   the closing (summary and thanks).

A format was recommended in order to establish a standard procedure across all interviews. Only responses from a non-managerial perspective were recorded. To gain insight into managers' opinion of the work environment as well as create a non-threatening atmosphere, the researcher asked conversational questions ("B1") during the formal line of inquiry ("B2" questions). Questions like "Do you believe you have been treated with dignity and respect during this period of strategic change in the organization" and "Do you feel that some of your peers have benefited more from the Management's Agenda for Strategic Change (MASC) than you have" were used. The interview questions were designed using formative and summative input for validation purposes.

Part A of the Interview Guide included participant information: Interviewee identification number, job title, location, gender, employee age, years in the industry, and years in the particular media organization. Part B of the Interview Guide included seven interview questions addressing issues of trust, fairness, and the management of change using an organizational justice framework. Summative input was obtained through face-to-face interviews of SMEs with practical experience, namely two senior-level managers and two non-managerial employees from a large-sized organization who were present SME from a large media organization. The goal of the formative and summative interview evaluations was to develop questions appropriate for answering the research questions of the study. The interview question development process discussed above (i.e., formative and summative evaluation of the preliminary interview questions) was used to ensure the reliability and validity of the interview questions. Part C of the Interview Guide included additional data on psychological contract fulfillment and based on a scale, The Psychological Contract Fulfillment Scale first developed and used by Henderson, Wayne, Shore, Bommer, and Tetrick (2008). The instructions to the participants were: "Please respond spontaneously with the first thoughts that come to mind upon hearing the following statements." This scale was developed as part of an investigation to highlight how Leader–Member Exchange (LMX) and psychological contract fulfillment processes work to shape the attitudes and behaviors of employees (Henderson et al., 2008: 1208).

Data Collection, Processing, and Analysis

Recommendations have also been made to use multiple sources of information during data collection to explore the range of historical, attitudinal, and behavioral issues related to the phenomena under study. The researcher collected data from this qualitative study through open-ended, semi-structured interview questions. Face and construct validity and formative evaluation of interview questions were assured through SME evaluation and pilot testing. The SMEs for this process consisted of one Ph.D. in English, one Ph.D. in Management, one Ph.D. in Human Resources, and two non-managerial employees who meet the sampling criteria of the study participants but are employed at another media organization other than the one under study.

First, a pilot study was conducted as a basis for confirming the applicability and dependability of the research questions and data collection techniques of the research. Three participants were selected through purposive and snowball sampling. These participants had knowledge of the research purpose. Since the individual interviews were the primary data gathering instrument for this research, a semi-structured interview was used in which questions were carefully designed to provide adequate coverage for the purpose of the research. The research questions were piloted with the three employees. The goal of the pilot study was to identify ambiguities, helped to clarify the wording of questions, and allowed for early detection of necessary additions or omissions. Participants in the pilot study were not interviewed in the full study, and data for the pilot study was not included as part of the full research.

In the full research, the participants selected for the interviews were a criterion sample of eight current employees from a media organization located in Nicosia, Cyprus. An attempt was made to select interview participants from each department within the organization. Using this approach the researcher ensured employees were represented from every department within the organization. Multiple cases were included within this study precisely to test for similar results (replication) across several cases. Replication across cases in the data collection from among the employees in this case study provided for confidence in the overall results and interpretations. Once the results from the data collection became repetitive, there may be no need to continue data collection as data saturation had been reached. Data saturation is achieved from the participant sample size. Two stages were proposed as a guide in order to make sure that saturation is achieved: an initial sample of 10 cases followed by a further three cases to determine if any new themes emerge. This research used a sample of eight employees to achieve data saturation.

The descriptive phase of data collection and analysis builds a foundation for interpretation when meanings are extracted from the data, comparisons are made, conceptual frameworks for interpretation are developed, conclusions are drawn, significance is determined, and, in some cases, theory is generated. Researchers have discovered that cases are bounded by activity and time, and researchers collect detailed information using a variety of data collection procedures. For the purpose of this qualitative multiple-case study, data collection was based on participants' responses to semi-structured interview questions.

Sufficient data was collected to produce confirmatory evidence that incorporates efforts directed at examining major rival explanations. To realize this aim, this research involved open-ended, semi-structured interviews for collecting participants' responses. Transformation of data into findings entailed grouping and organization of descriptive findings in a way that facilitated the analysis and reporting of employees' perceptions of trust, fairness, and the management of change using an organizational justice framework. The researcher combined the formulated research questions, insights, and interpretations that emerge from the study. Prompted questions were grouped with any spontaneous, naturally occurring statements provided by participants.

Different data collection approaches were used with each of the case studies to understand participants' perceptions and experiences. Data collection involved gathering the eight participants' responses during in-depth, face-to-face semi-structured interviews with a digital recording device. Handwritten field notes were developed during interview sessions to capture participants' key responses and actions. Interview sessions were digitally recorded using an Olympus Digital Recorder, Model VN-7700. This digital recorder was selected because it had multiple functions, such as voice-activated recording, dictation correction, variable speed playback, track marking, and file splitting for easy handling of long recording, and also because it was portable and convenient to operate.

A comprehensive case study database is necessary for replicating case study research and ensuring quality control. The research included the use of Microsoft® Excel spreadsheets for sole access and the storing, organization, and tracking of participants' contact information on the basis of the numerical classification system used to identify them. Microsoft® Excel spreadsheets were also used to track schedules and meeting arrangements with participants so as to set up the eight individual face-to-face interview sessions. The Excel spreadsheets were stored on a personal computer that has back-up systems for the protection of data and files that have been electronically generated.

Qualitative data collected through content analysis of interviews were thematically coded. The identified themes were used for data triangulation. Data triangulation was used to corroborate facts found within the multiple data sources. To facilitate data management, the interview notes were organized by the research questions and sub-questions. Themes were organized by a number and letter combination, with the number referring to the research question number and the letter referring to a distinct theme. For example, the second theme in Research Question Q2 was identified as Theme 2B, whereas the third theme in Research Question Q3 was identified as Theme 3C. Most recorded interview sessions lasted no longer than one hour.

Digitally recorded interview sessions were transcribed into Microsoft® Excel spreadsheet software, organized by participant number, and uploaded into NVivo (Version 9) qualitative software for purposes of coding and analysis. NVivo was chosen for this study because the software enables qualitative researchers to easily code, track, organize, and analyze data. In addition, NVivo was used to assist in identifying themes. Tables or matrices were developed to display themes. Potential variations in data accuracy and errors were identified and noted in the research.

Eight interview transcriptions (i.e., one transcription per participant) formatted in Microsoft® Word documents were used as the sole data source uploaded in NVivo. By using NVivo, specific words and phrases were extracted from transcriptions, which enabled the researcher to arrive at a better understanding of the results. Case notes were created in NVivo to assign numerical identification to each of the eight participants' transcriptions. NVivo is used to track unique nodes, words, and textural descriptors or phrases throughout the transcripts. The use of notes enabled content to be gathered easily from each case. Confidentiality was protected because the notes did not indicate participants' identities.

Identified themes were consistent, referenced, and traceable to the data collected. Keywords were extracted from the data. Thematic analysis of the multiple cases was used in this study to perform the content analysis including the identification of themes and exploration of perceptions from multiple cases. Content analysis also provides a basis for quantifying data for the purposes of future research. The process of content analysis was used to identify, code, and differentiate primary patterns of data for each case. Each theme identified was analyzed to describe the phenomena being investigated. Data was analyzed to identify trends and to differentiate between inconsistencies in results. Lastly, narratives have been developed to describe the themes.

Research results were analyzed to identify recurring themes or words that participants articulated during the interview process. Participants' responses recorded in transcriptions were coded by headings and interview questions. Furthermore, data were coded to identify emerging patterns and have been compared to other coded categories to assess linkages and meanings between cases, as suggested by Patton (2002). An analysis of interview results provided insights regarding linkages between respondent data and management theories that were described in this study.

By triangulating with multiple data sources, observers, methods, and/or theories, researchers can make significant strides in overcoming skepticism that meets singular methods, lone analysts, and single-perspective interpretations. Triangulation was used by collecting information from multiple sources to corroborate the facts. Different methodologies were used in this study to establish triangulation and validate participants' intended meanings. Field notes were written during interviews to capture participants' key responses, emotions, actions, and themes, which may not appear in transcripts. Throughout the interview process, field notes were a secondary method of gathering data. A technique adapted from Groenewald (2004) was used to collect field notes adhering to the process listed below:

1.   Observational notes taken in order to record events as they actually happened during the interview.

2.   Notes were taken which reflected the initial interpretation concerning meanings.

3.   Methodological notes were written in order to remind the researcher to do certain things at the right time.

4.   Memos were taken at the end of each interview session to develop brief abstract summaries.

Interview transcriptions were analyzed to assess patterns and themes that emerged from each participant interview and were compared to field notes for further corroboration and verification. Further triangulation took place in this study by providing participants with their interview transcripts and requesting their feedback regarding the accuracy and validity of the transcribed material.

Cross-case synthesis was the analytical technique used to aggregate results across case studies. Cross-case synthesis applies to the analysis of two or more cases. By using cross-case synthesis for data analysis, it will be possible to determine whether the results of the case studies are comparable. The more cases that are included, the more robust the results will be. For the purpose of the current study, the researcher conducted a cross-case synthesis on eight in-depth, face-to-face interviews; each case study provided strong evidence and a base for analyzing how an organizational justice framework can be used to explore and understand employees' perceptions of trust, fairness, and the management of change in a media organization based in Cyprus. Each individual case in the cross-case synthesis was treated as a separate case, but synthesis of the data from each case strengthened the robustness of the study's results.

Assumptions

This multiple-case study was based on various assumptions. One assumption is that participants provided in-depth perspectives and opinions regarding factors that could enhance understanding of how an organizational justice framework can be used to explore employees' perceptions of trust, fairness, and the management of change during a period of strategic change in a privately-owned media organization based in Cyprus. Another assumption was that participants provided honest responses to each interview question asked by the researcher. A further assumption was that digitally recorded interview sessions for the eight participants were accurately transcribed. Following, another assumption was that by using a representation of the data set of variables, displaying the information in analytical tools such as NVivo, meaningful information was extracted to Word documents to support the research of this study.

Limitations

The major limitation of this study was the fact that only one privately-owned media organization that is undergoing a strategic change in Cyprus was examined. However, the methodology that was developed and tested during the study could also be used by other media organizations in Cyprus that are undergoing strategic change to explore employees' perceptions of trust, fairness, and the management of change using an organizational justice framework. Another limitation for this study was that it depended on the selected subjects volunteering their time to take part in the interviews, and that the media organization's prevailing environment may influence the sample population to answer in a particular way.

Since respondents were asked to verbalize and explain their perceptions of trust, fairness, and the management of change, some bias may emerge in the research findings. Participants were asked to provide specific information regarding the media organization where they work; participants may have had biases about employers' competitive advantages or competitors, which could affect perspectives and perceptions. The possibility of bias and misinterpretation of results was limited, because the researcher digitally recorded and transcribed each interview accurately in order to document participants' responses.

Researchers argue that participants may have different perceptions that stem from cultural background, work experiences, educational level, and knowledge of employers' competitive positions in the workplace. In addition, some participants expressed biases as a result of conflicting schedules or time limitations to responding fully to interview questions. In order to help overcome this potential limitation, the researcher scheduled interviews during times that were most convenient for participants and ensured the interview questions could all be covered within the allotted time. The latter was investigated during the pilot study.

Another limitation for this study was that the research would not be repeated at a later time to compare results with initial findings. Other researchers who will read the results of this study may be willing to perform future studies in other cities or countries regarding the exploration of employees' perceptions of trust, fairness, and the management of change during a period of strategic change using an organizational justice framework. The researcher also recognized that economic trends in the media environment, internally and externally, could influence study participants' perceptions regarding factors that affected their perceptions of trust, fairness, and the management of change.

Researchers must also consider how statements, behaviors, and relationships with participants may influence research results. The interviewer has the responsibility to create an environment in which the research participant will feel comfortable and will respond comprehensively and honestly to each question. Other researchers have ascertained that participants who feel comfortable with the interviewer are more likely to share information and express their perceptions. The researcher encouraged open communication with the participants and clarified the meaning of the research process and interview questions in order to support positive relations with the respondents.

Delimitations

A delimitation of this study involved the targeted participant population. Only individuals who are non-managerial employees of the media organization in Cyprus were solicited to participate in this study. To help achieve a generalized sample, one or two participants from each department, based on the number of employees of each department, of the specific media organization were interviewed. This delimitation helped provide a mix of perceptions from participants who work in different departments of the media organization.

Chapter 7

The Case Study

Findings

The purpose of this qualitative study was to examine how an organizational justice framework can be used to explore employees' perceptions of trust, fairness, and the management of change during a period of strategic change in a privately-owned media organization based in Cyprus. A multiple-case study research design was used to satisfy the goal of this exploratory research, with data collected through multiple sources, including in-depth individual interviews, field notes, and SME review and reflection of the data collected. Following, SME examination on the subject matter provided formative evaluation of the interview guide/instrument and SME reflection on the data collected provided an unbiased and objective view in the analysis phase.

A qualitative multiple-case study design was used in this study to focus on eight in-depth, face-to-face interviews with employees from a media organization located in Cyprus. The criteria for selection included non-managerial employees who had at least three years of work experience in the media organization. Four participants were currently active in sales, two were carrying out responsibilities as technicians, and two were carrying out responsibilities as cameramen in the particular media organization in Nicosia, Cyprus. All eight participants had good and ample information on the issues under study. Data collection involved gathering the eight participants' responses during in-depth, face-to-face semi-structured interviews with a digital recording device. In addition, handwritten field notes were taken during interview sessions to capture participants' key responses and actions.

The results, findings, and summaries of participant responses are provided to describe employees' perceptions of trust, fairness, and the management of change during a period of strategic change in a privately-owned media organization based in Cyprus, using an organizational justice framework. Comparisons between theoretical framework and actual findings are described to indicate any differences and knowledge gained from this study. This research focused on the following central research question:

Q1   How can an organizational justice framework be used to explore employees' perceptions of trust, fairness, and the management of change within the context of strategic change?

The sub-questions derived from the central questions are:

Q2   How can an organizational justice framework be used to explore employees' perceptions of trust within the context of strategic change?

Q3   How can an organizational justice framework be used to explore employees' perceptions of fairness within the context of strategic change?

Q4   How can an organizational justice framework be used to explore employees' perceptions of the management of change within the context of strategic change?

Evaluations of the findings have been provided and focus on participants' responses to the following semi-structured interview questions that were used in this study:

1.   Did management inform employees with a thorough explanation of the MASC before enacting its agenda? If yes, did you believe the explanation was reasonable and accurate?

2.   Have you been able to express your views and feelings during the MASC?

3.   How fair has your organization been in rewarding you when you consider the responsibilities you have been assigned since the MASC?

4.   Do you believe you have been treated with dignity and respect during this period of strategic change in the organization?

5.   Since the enactment of the MASC, how do you perceive that your attitude towards your organization has been affected?

6.   Since the enactment of the MASC, how do you perceive that your attitude towards your peers has been affected?

7.   Do you feel that some of your peers have benefited more from the MASC than you have?

Following, participants provided supplemental data on psychological contract fulfillment based on an organizational justice framework, and responded spontaneously with the first thoughts that come to their mind upon hearing the following four statements.

1.   [My company] has often broken promises made to me.

2.   Considering the promises [my company] has made to me, the company hasn't always lived up to its end of the bargain. (reverse scored).

3.   [My company] has kept its promises to me.

4.   [My company] fulfills its obligations to me.

Summarized Results of the Pilot Study

The pilot study was conducted as a basis for confirming the applicability and dependability of the research questions and data collection techniques.

Three individuals were selected to conduct the pilot study in order to determine if the interview questions were valid. Following, are some detailed results from the three pilot study participants that were interviewed in the pilot study.

INTERVIEW #1

Participant A1 was 28 years old, male, and currently working as a cameraman in the media organization under study. He was nine years in the industry with four years in the media organization. Dependability and applicability were essential criteria for quality during the interview, and the researcher managed to enhance the dependability of qualitative research. With the use of questions asked, the researcher increased understanding and revealed insights regarding employees' perceptions of trust, fairness, and the management of change using an organizational justice framework. The interview questions did supply the data expected to answer the study's research questions.

INTERVIEW #2

Participant A2 was 42 years old, male, and was currently working in the sales department of the media organization. He had been in the industry for 15 years and working in the media organization for 12 years. To ensure validity and reliability in the pilot study, the researcher studied multiple cases. Again here, the researcher managed to gather information in order to understand and reveal insights regarding employees' perceptions of trust, fairness, and the management of change using an organizational justice framework. The interview questions did supply the data expected to answer the study's research questions.

INTERVIEW #3

Participant A3 was a 36 year old female, who was currently working in the sales department of the media organization. She was 10 years in the industry and working for seven years in the media organization. Semi-structured questions were used in this pilot study to guide participants in expressing in-depth perceptions. The interview questions did supply the data expected to answer the study's research questions.

Finally, on the issue of any potential occupational risks that might have incurred since participants were current employees of this organization under study and were asked potentially sensitive topics, all three participants expressed experiencing trust and safety in the interview and towards the researcher. All were informed they could stop the interview at any time. No one participant stopped the interview or expressed any hesitation during the interview process. Actually, two out of the three expressed feeling positive about being open and honest with the researcher about these issues and believed their views need to be heard through the research study.

Results of the Main Study

Interview sessions were conducted in one face-to-face meeting with each of the eight participants. The researcher selected interview participants from each department within the organization in order to ensure all employees were represented. Interview sessions were digitally recorded and transcribed.

Handwritten field notes were taken during interview sessions to capture participants' key responses and actions. To maintain participants' anonymity and confidentiality, participants were referred to by participant number in this study rather than by name.

The use of NVivo software allows qualitative researchers to code data for well-established results analysis. Interview session transcriptions were drawn up in Microsoft® Word documents, according to participant number, and uploaded into NVivo (Version 9) software for data analysis. A search of frequently occurring words in the transcriptions revealed the emergence of different themes. The use of notes enabled content to be gathered easily from each case. To organize the eight participants' transcriptions in a numerical identification system as well as enable easy access to each file, case nodes were created in NVivo. This program was used to track unique nodes, words, and textural descriptors or phrases throughout the transcripts. The particular method provided the researcher with insights into patterns, unique and reoccurring themes, and linked research results, all of which are noted and documented as appropriate. Offering increased understanding of results, text search queries in NVivo revealed frequently occurring words expressed by participants. Examples of frequently occurring words were:

a)   fairness;

b)   strategic change;

c)   trust;

d)   communication;

e)   management;

f)   commitment; and

g)   unfairness.

DEMOGRAPHIC FINDINGS

The participants for the current study were eight non-managerial employees of a large-sized, privately owned media organization based in Nicosia, Cyprus. The participants had suitable knowledge on the subject of media management. The eight in-depth interviews were conducted in order to gain understanding of employees' perceptions of fairness, trust, and the management of change using the organizational justice framework, in a media organization undergoing change. Following, there was no single department in the organization that was over represented in the sample; there were five males and four females, with an age range from 22 to 55 years old. Study participants had at least three years of work experience in the media organization, and were currently active in sales or carrying out responsibilities as technicians or cameramen. The participants' years of experience within the media industry ranged from three to 14 years.

RESULTS OF SEMI-STRUCTURED INTERVIEWS

Seven interview questions were developed to support the findings of the overarching research question and subsequent sub-questions. To acknowledge relevant perceptions of trust, fairness, and the management of change during organizational change in a media organization in Cyprus using an organizational justice framework, unique questions were provided in research results to indicate supporting themes that emerged from participant interview sessions. Transcription results from interview sessions indicated significant themes. Triangulation was then performed utilizing field notes and SME reflection on the data. Research question findings are noted below based on specific interview questions in the qualitative case study.

SUB-QUESTION I

How can an organizational justice framework be used to explore employees' perceptions of trust within the context of strategic change?

To address the first sub-question, participants were asked questions to identify how they feel since the enactment of the MASC and how do they perceive that their attitude towards their organization, and or towards their peers has been affected. Interview questions #5 and #6 corresponded to this research sub-question and participant responses are detailed below.

FINDINGS FOR INTERVIEW QUESTION #5

Participants' responses to interview question #5, since the enactment of the MASC how do you perceive that your attitude towards your organization has been affected, revealed three emergent themes. These were trust, organizational relationships, and commitment. The following is an overview of participants' perspectives regarding these themes.

Trust

Seven out of eight participants (87.5 percent) believed that their attitude towards their organization has been affected, as related to trust, since the enactment of the MASC in the media organization. Since the enactment of the MASC the organization did not communicate honestly with their employees, and as a result trust eroded leading to doubt and confusion internally (Participant #1; Participant #5; Participant #6). Participant #2 explained:

> In times of change, management needs to understand how and what it takes to create the vital elements of trust between managers and employees. I still do not understand why our management didn't establish and maintain the integrity by keeping their promises and telling us the truth and what's really going to happen. I do not trust the organization and the management anymore, they do not communicate their opinions and ideas to us, and my attitude has changed too towards the organization in a negative way. I'm not willing to work with passion as before. Management tells us half-truths, or nothing. How are we supposed to trust them?

Participant #7 stated that:

> The organization must give us the permission to express our concerns and feelings in constructive ways. During this difficult period that we are going through now, we are all anxious and vulnerable, and we are in pain. With management's current position towards us, I do not care about the needs of the business, because the business does not seem to care about us. No trust in the management, and no interest in my work anymore.

According to Participant #4:

> My attitude towards my organization changed because management does not talk to us straight, is not honest, and sometimes they do not demonstrate any respect. Trust disappeared from the members in our workplace, and you can realize this because they are not willing to work hard, and as a result goals are not accomplished. The only thing management does is to waste time in meetings or put further pressure on employees to increase productivity to meet organizational goals. But, when there is no trust, goals will never be achieved.

Participant #8 mentioned the significance of information sharing in the workplace in order for employees to continue having trust in management, since communication supports the information and willingness to interact with employees during times of uncertainty and ambiguity. "Trust affects the quality of relationships and this is what we are experiencing now, since the attitude of a lot of our peers have changed negatively towards management, and in some situations towards their colleagues" (Participant #6).

Organizational relationships

Three out of eight participants (37.5 percent) believed that their attitude towards their organization has been affected, in relation to the interactions they have with their manager, since the enactment of the MASC in the media organization. Participant #4 explained:

> My attitude and my behavior are influenced in a negative way because the interaction I have with my manager is becoming very complicated. I don't trust my manager, and we can't develop a healthy organizational relationship. Working together with your manager or with your colleagues requires trust, and I often question whether my manager has the relevant skills and knowledge to handle this change with their subordinates.

Similarly, Participant #6 believed that:

> When employees trust their managers they will be very supportive of the organization during change, even willing to work for more hours without expecting more money. My attitude towards the organization changed because I don't trust the organization as before, and employees' relationships with the organization changed because there is limited trust. Management must sit down and examine why trust failed, which leads to negative organizational relationships.

Participant #7 stated that:

> Senior management must recognize the actions that cause trust to fail between managers and employees. When trust erodes, employees feel insecure, they are less productive and committed, and organizational relationships with managers and employees erode too. My trust towards the organization failed because management refused any kind of specific

information and do not provide us with support and guidance when we needed it.

Commitment

All eight participants (100 percent) believed that their attitude towards their organization has been affected since the enactment of the MASC in the media organization, quoting commitment as one of the most important factors related to the success of strategic changes. Some participants believed that when employees feel committed in their workplace this helps in the development of a very good environment, especially in the context of change (Participant #3; Participant #4; Participant #7; Participant #8). Participant #3 explained that:

I would be more committed to the organization if management showed more willingness to cooperate with us. We have no leaders in this organization, because if we had leaders, they would understand and promote commitment, which is an essential element for the effective implementation of the strategic change initiative. I also experienced some unfair situations that have to do with colleagues being promoted (during this time of changes) to positions that had nothing to do with their previous responsibilities, and this makes me less committed to the organization.

Participant #2 stated:

If I felt more committed I wouldn't want to leave the organization because of the changes taking place. Because I don't feel committed I'm more stressed and I don't want to go to work in the morning. This change brought a lot of changes to my current job, like heavier workload and increased role ambiguity, because now I do everything; one day my manager may tell me to go to see some clients, and the other day I might be asked to do something totally different. This is a reason to be less committed, and less dedicated to my job.

Participant #1 stated:

At the beginning, I was positive to change, although I did not have any official communication from the management. Later, management started changing our roles and areas of responsibilities without asking us or at least having a short discussion before assigning us the new roles; I experienced anxiety, loss of control, and confusion. I was expecting to have clear information but it was just a wish that was never implemented. Now, I'm very pessimistic about this change and my commitment to the organization is less. I don't feel positive about the change.

"When management fails in communicating change, rumors and resistance to change, including strikes, will be part of the strategic change" (Participant #5). "Less commitment and more fear are the results of bad communication and not adequate leadership" (Participant #6). "My attitude changed towards the organization because of the uncertainty about my future within the organization and the fact that psychologically I feel very bad" (Participant #4). Participant #7 believed that, "In times of changes within the organization it is expected that employees' attitudes will be negatively changed if the organization keeps a distance from them and does not consider them in their decisions." Participant #2 noted, "During this change I am more attentive to how I am treated by my manager, especially in regards to fairness."

FINDINGS FOR INTERVIEW QUESTION #6

Participant responses to interview question #6, since the enactment of the MASC how do you perceive that your attitude towards your peers has been affected, provided insights into three emergent themes. These covered teamwork, trust, and communication. The following is a summary overview of participants' perspectives regarding these themes.

Teamwork

Five out of eight participants (62.5 percent) believed that their attitudes towards their peers have changed, and now they are less willing to work in team efforts. Participant #4 explained:

After change, it is more difficult for me to work in teams as I effectively used to do before. My work position requires teamwork because we have a wide range of responsibilities, such as cross-functional teams or self-managing teams, and the goal is to improve the production process. Teamwork was part of the culture of this organization because in my department we had some collective tasks where the team members were mutually regulating the execution of these collective tasks, which now I'm not willing to do. I do not blame my colleagues, I blame the management of my organization, but even if I don't want to behave like this, my attitude changed towards my peers too.

On the other hand, Participant #8 asserted:

> *Currently, I can't say that my attitude towards my peers has been affected nor it remained the same. Some years ago, we used to be a high performance organization having a lot of power and influence in the media industry. This was because we were always working in teams, having great support from our managers, because our work requires a broader scope of knowledge, expertise, and judgment. What I can say is that, the advantage of teamwork is significant in the increase in productivity, which requires creative resolution of different tasks, and I'm willing to work in teams like before with my colleagues. In times of change, teamwork must create an environment that can facilitate knowledge and information exchange inside our organization, something that is not implemented now.*

According to Participant #3:

> *My attitudes have changed negatively towards my peers because now no one takes responsibilities, and many experience low levels of job satisfaction. Employees do not have direct participation in the organizational changes, and they are not willing to work in teams, or if they are obliged to get involved in teamwork, they are not productive.*

Participant #2 stated:

> *Since the enactment of the MASC my attitudes have changed positively towards my peers because I feel closer to them now, and more willing to work as a team and share information and knowledge. I think that employees are more flexible and willing to work together, trying to build a culture where everyone can be part of the team.*

As Participant #5 stated:

> *Personally my attitude towards my peers has changed since the last organizational changes, I don't trust my colleagues and management. My work requires trust and being able to work in teams. Currently, employees are not willing to improve their skills and cooperate amongst themselves, because they don't feel secure in the workplace and they are ruled by fear. I consider normal our attitudes to change towards our peers too, we are humans not machines.*

Trust

Seven out of eight participants (87.5 percent) believed that their attitudes towards their peers have changed, as related to trust. Participant #1 believed that the need for collaborative relationships in times of change could benefit the organization:

> I believe that my attitude towards my colleagues didn't change, and I always advise my peers that passive behaviors and neglectful activities will not help our organization to be successful in this change initiative, but will drive the organization to failure.

Participant #6 stated:

> I understand that effective changes can only be achieved with trust among employees who are the driving forces that will facilitate and sustain effective change in an organization. My attitude towards my peers has not been affected to a large degree, but I feel that I don't trust them as before. The reason is that I see some behaviors inside the organization by my peers that prove that most employees look at how to save themselves, and are not willing to cooperate with their colleagues. I don't blame them, but how can my behavior not change when I see that their attitude towards me has changed, because of the changes that are taking place in the organization?

Participant #2 believed that, "Attitudes always change in times of strategic change, because of the perceptions of fairness of organizational decision-making. This also has an impact on an employee's attitude towards not only the management, but also their peers." Participant #5 believed:

> My attitude towards my peers, since the enactment of the MASC, has changed because I feel insecure and this change is a threat, and trust towards my peers has been reduced. I do not trust my peers as before because this change involves restructuring, job cuts, salary changes, and I see that my colleagues' attitudes changed too towards other colleagues. Before change, we used to be like a family, now we are trying to survive on top of others.

Another participant stated that, "When employees adopt a negative attitude this harms people around them and can cause people stress and boredom"

(Participant #3). "On the other hand, a thankful and positive attitude like the one I adopt towards my peers promotes trust, and a positive working environment that help to reinforce specific behaviors" (Participant #8). Participant #4 asserted that, "When employees have a negative attitude then that attitude will be reflected through their behavior. Because of the change, employees adopt a pessimistic attitude, which affects the quality of employees' work and the trust between them."

Communication

Four out of eight participants (50 percent) believed that since the enactment of the MASC their attitudes towards their peers have changed, as related to the communication between them. "Since the enactment of the strategic change in the workplace a lot of employees acquired new attitudes and behaviors including towards managers, and communication has been decreased" (Participant #6). Participant #1 asserted that:

> I think that employees who had positive attitudes before the enactment of any organizational change, and who adopt negative attitudes after change are not doing anything particularly wrong. I've noticed a lot of negative attitudes from our peers after change but what I understand is that employees have this cynical and negative feeling because of the insecurity they feel in the workplace and because of the fact that the organization does not provide to employees a consistent communication. My attitude has changed to a relatively small degree towards my peers, but still we do not communicate on a regular basis as before the enactment of the change. I feel that we keep a distance between us, there is a lot of stress and in some situations some of my colleagues ignore me when I ask for their help in my work.

As Participant #3 stated:

> My attitude changed towards my peers because there is no communication between my peers in my department. My colleagues adopted new attitudes and they hold a distance between each other; I tried at the beginning to be friendly with them and show them that we can work through this change together as a team, as we were acting before the change, but it seems that their attitude will not change if they do not feel secure about their job.

Communication between employees during changes helps in avoiding negative attitudes and behaviors in the workplace (Participant #4; Participant #2). Participant #3 asserted that:

> *After the enactment of change and during the process of change in organizations, the organization itself must enrich its communication practices between management and between employees in order to avoid negative attitudes and shape positive ones. My attitudes changed because my peers' attitudes changed in a negative way, and this is because of the absence of communication between the employees.*

SUB-QUESTION 2

How can an organizational justice framework be used to explore employees' perceptions of fairness within the context of strategic change?

To determine the second sub-question, participants were asked questions to identify whether they were able to express their views and feelings during the MASC, and how fair has their organization been in rewarding them when they consider the responsibilities they have been assigned since the MASC. In addition, participants were also asked to identify if they believe they have been treated with dignity and respect during the period of strategic change in the organization, and whether they feel that some of their peers have benefited more from the MASC than they have. Interview questions #2, #3, #4, and #7 corresponded to this research sub-question and participant responses are detailed below.

FINDINGS FOR INTERVIEW QUESTION #2

Participants' responses to interview question #2, have you been able to express your views and feelings during the MASC, revealed four emergent themes: organizational support, performance and employee turnover, organizational commitment, and behavioral change. The following is an overview of participants' perspectives regarding these themes.

Organizational support

Four out of eight participants (50 percent) believed that when employees are treated in a way that they can express their views and feelings during organizational change, this might lead to organizational support and trustworthy behavior on the part of employees towards managers. Participant

#1 believed that employees' perceptions and feelings have to be seriously considered by management, especially in times of change, and employees have to be asked by management about these since they can solve any kind of disputes or conflicts within the organization. Specifically, Participant #1 stated:

> *No one from the management asked us if we consider right or wrong the organization's decision, or even to listen to our suggestions. We weren't able to express our feelings regarding the organization's policies during this change. As a result, our reactions towards the organization were negative since any decisions were taken directly by the organization without our input, even to be able to express our opinions or ideas for this change. This is why a lot of employees are not willing now to offer support to the organization in their try for change. I know employees who refuse to cooperate even with their colleagues.*

Participant #5 added that transparency of the processes by which decisions are made can lead to fair outcomes for employees, when their suggestions are heard by the management, and this can lead to organizational support for organizational change. "If management have asked for our opinion during change then this change could have been turned to be successful in the long term, but I personally do not think that the change outcomes will be positive" (Participant #5). Participant #7 stated:

> *Employees' views and feelings during MASC have a direct impact on organizational support from the employees towards the organization. The use of such fair procedures helps employees to have a say in the decision process in the workplace, and employees must have a voice to express their feelings in times of change. This promotes fairness in the workplace where employees express their perceptions of fairness regarding outcomes, and by this employees have more input in the appraisal process. Also, employees could support the organization when the management hears their "voice" and we could be more positive to this change and overall have a positive impact on outcomes.*

As Participant #8 asserted, "when employees are given the opportunity to express their views and feelings during change this can promote organizational support and employees' acceptance of change outcomes even when these are seen as unfavorable." Participant #2 asserted:

> *In times of change people get frustrated and organizations must have charismatic leaders. This currently does not happen in our organization,*

and it seems that management failed to keep together and unite their employees. Management didn't ask about our views during change, they didn't even bother to communicate to us the reasons for the changes in a way that we can understand the context, the purpose, and the need. Now, they expect from us to support the organization in their effort for change, tell me how this is possible? And how fair does it sound to an employee who sacrificed 11 years of his life in this organization? They nearly destroyed our credibility towards the organization because they provide us incorrect and insufficient information, and the most important, they don't listen. And if they listen, answers are given too quickly, and rumor is already in action, which leads us not to trust them anymore.

According to Participant #3 and Participant #6, some employees were able to express their opinions to the management during MASC, and they were two of them. Participant #3 considered these actions as fair on behalf of management and an opportunity for employees to be heard and have their views. Following, Participant #6 stated:

As understanding and acceptance are important determinants of an employee's behavior in times of change, by expressing our views it helped us increase our support towards the organization and our colleagues. We are willing to work more effectively in teamwork and help our organization implement this change successfully.

Participant #4 indicated that:

The importance of feedback from employees to management, and communication between employees during change in the workplace, could help our organization to successfully implement this change.

Performance and employee turnover

Six out of eight participants (75 percent) believed that employees must express their views and feelings during the MASC as this has an impact on performance and employee turnover. Some participants stated that their beliefs regarding how decisions on actions are made may have a positive impact on the degree of organizational performance and employee turnover (Participant #1; Participant #4; Participant #8). Participant #2 stated:

For the past nine months the organization stopped giving us any kind of information or asking for our opinion, and we were not able to express our feelings about the changes taking place. Here we are talking about strategic changes, structural changes, reductions in our salaries by 25%–30% from one day to another, or even changing our tasks and responsibilities because they fired employees and we need to fill those positions too, with a lower salary. This has a negative impact on our behavior within the workplace, like lower productivity and performance (poor services), bad rumors, and lower quality of services in our work. A large number of dissatisfied employees are under physical disturbance such as tension, depression, and sleeplessness. Therefore, it is necessary for the organization to place the fairness of those actions in high consideration and give us more freedom of expression of our views and thoughts.

Participant #3 asserted that employees are rarely asked to express their opinions and ideas during the MASC and that management frequently asked them to change jobs because of the lay-offs of employees within the organization. "The results of employees not being able to express their views and feelings during the MASC may result in poor services and performance, and employee dissatisfaction," as stated by Participant #5.

Organizational commitment

Six out of eight participants (75 percent) believed that employees must express their views and feelings during the MASC as this has an impact on organizational commitment. As Participant #7 stated:

Management cannot cope with this unexpected change, they didn't ask us how we perceive change and if we had any suggestions to make this change go more smoothly. I am working seven years in this organization, and I believe that my performance 'til now is very good but since management ignores my presence and my views, I can't employ positive behavioral actions anymore in the workplace environment. My level of commitment is low and I feel that my organization's future is uncertain and unpredictable.

Participant #8 believed:

We understand that executives, senior managers, and middle managers are faced with considerable pressure this period to improve the financial performance of our organization and keep as many work positions "alive" as possible. But, because they didn't involve employees' opinions in their decisions, they make this change process more difficult. By just announcing the cutting of the costs, downsizing, and restructuring of departments and assets this change will fail. They need our support, and we need them next to us, communicating with us, and listening to our suggestions and ideas. The core of change is people, is us, is everyone working within the media organization. We can build together key strategies to promote change, and we will survive. Feeling involved in this effort we can be more committed and more willing to support our organization.

Participant #1 stated:

Employee attitude and behavior is associated with the way the organization is facing their employees. If the organization asks for employees' views and understands their feelings, this will have a positive effect on organizational commitment and the positive behavior towards the organization, from the side of the employees.

Similarly, Participant #4 asserted:

I'm working for seven years in this organization and I'm really glad that at this moment I still have my job. I wasn't able to express my views and feelings during the MASC, but I understand that the current period that we are facing is a challenge period, that we as employees must generate dynamism and be able to manage the situation in a positive way. By adopting negative behaviors this can cause even more harm to the organization and to our health. If we want to keep our organization "alive" and stay competitive in the rapidly changing market, the least we can do is to be committed in our work and stay close as employees.

According to Participant #6:

When employees are not able to express their views during these tremendous changes that are taking place in our workplace environment, they will report lower satisfaction and commitment with management, lower trust, and for sure decreased job security. Personally, I wake up and I go to my office and every time the phone rings, I get stressed because I feel that is maybe the Human Resources (HR) manager and he wants to see me in his office to announce that I'm fired. Imagine having this feeling every single moment of the day, how do they expect us to be productive and committed when management reacts like this?

Participant #3 noted:

> *When organizations consider their members during change and ask for their opinions and feelings during the change process, this is considered to be fair and plays an important role for the success of the change, and employees are more likely to commit to a change if they perceive the process to be fair.*

Behavioral change

Three out of eight participants (37.5 percent) believed that when employees are treated in a way that they can express their views and feelings during organizational change, this might be a reason to positively change their behavior and adapt more easily to change. Participant #2 stated:

> *If management asked for our views and feelings, let's say on a weekly basis, then they wouldn't have a hard time dealing with change. Employees' behaviors would be more easily adapted to these difficult circumstances and we, as employees, could be more positive to these changes.*

As Participant #5 said:

> *The organization itself created multiple barriers between managers and employees, and now there is no collaboration and teamwork to the degree it had to be inside the organization and this makes it more complex for the management to achieve their goals. Employee behaviors changed negatively towards management and they rarely maintain interpersonal relationships to the level that is required to ensure success in the change initiative. Management should have been more close with employees and use us (as employees) to help them achieve the planned change, by changing the way we think, the way we react, and generally the way we behave in a positive way.*

Participant #7 believed that top management did not provide specific guidelines and strategy to be followed by middle managers to lead employees through the change, and this is why employees are not able to express their views or are asked to express their feelings during change.

> *Managers should hold individual meetings with each single employee from their department and ask them to express their views, because*

> *this one-on-one interaction helps employees to understand better the change strategy and adopt their behavior to this change, helping the organization to succeed*

FINDINGS FOR INTERVIEW QUESTION #3

Participants' responses to interview question #3, how fair has your organization been in rewarding you when you consider the responsibilities you have been assigned since the MASC, revealed three emergent themes. These covered lower productivity, trust, and job dissatisfaction. The following is an overview of participants' perspectives regarding these themes.

Lower productivity

Seven out of eight participants (87.5 percent) believed that when employees' perceptions of fairness of rewards and responsibilities that have been assigned since the MASC are considered to be unfair, then the level of productivity falls. Participant #1 stated:

> *The organization announced a 25%–30% salary cut off and has assigned me with extra responsibilities. I'm actually working more hours per week, having more responsibilities, and I feel that my productivity level is lower than before now. I know that I'm not rewarded as before and I feel that the new responsibilities that I've been assigned and the level of pay are not considered to be fair. How can I be willing to make the organizational change a success when the management is treating me like this?*

Employees should perceive that the new responsibilities assigned and the level of pay they receive are considered to be fair, otherwise productivity will be below average (Participant #3; Participant #4; Participant #7). According to Participant #2:

> *According to my professional experience, my abilities, my education, and the effort I exert in my work, I expected to have had triple the salary I have now, be appreciated from the top management, and have better working conditions. Currently, I don't consider fair my rewards compared to the new responsibilities that I have since change has taken place in my organization, and as a result, I'm not working as passionately as I used to, I am psychologically tensed, and this does not motivate me to be productive. Top management acted unethically*

by decreasing our salaries, firing employees, and assigning us with extra responsibilities just to save money. They should have seen and considered their employees more seriously before they took any action on our salaries. Personally, I am not supporting the organization as I used to because they want us to work for more hours, have more responsibilities and get paid less. This is unfair and unethical.

As Participant #6 stated:

It was expected that our salaries would decrease, because of these changes we have in the economy and in a lot of organizations. We have to realize that if we want our organization to survive nowadays we have to be alert, flexible, and willing to change the way we behave and work. Offering less quality will not be a solution, being positive as a person will make a positive change day by day in the change process we are going through.

Participant #8 added that:

Because I understand the current situation we are going through, I consider fair the rewards as related to my new responsibilities assigned since the MASC, and I am very positive to work more and be more productive than before. Isolating ourselves from the management will not be a solution to this problem.

Trust

Four out of eight participants (50 percent) believed that when employees' perceptions of fairness on rewards and responsibilities that have been assigned since the MASC are considered to be fair, then they could trust the organization and the management. Participant #2 believed that the organization didn't reward its employees fairly even if they assigned them new responsibilities and longer work shifts. "This has a negative effect on our efficiency and productivity, and our trust towards management." Participant #7 asserted:

I do not consider fair the way management allocated the rewards after the reduction in salaries that was announced lately. I believe that salary reduction was not implemented on all levels, and that management assigned more tasks and responsibilities to the non-managerial employees with a reduced salary. Management believes that we will accept any percentage reduction in our salaries and be willing to accept also new responsibilities. This is unfair and unethical on the part of management. They are not honest and transparent with us and they don't demonstrate any kind of respect. They do not even apologize when they do mistakes. I don't trust management anymore, and I already started looking for another job.

Participant #3 believed that there was no comparison between their current salary (after reduction) with the new responsibilities that they undertook. "Employees feel uncertain and they do not trust the management. They consider management to be part of the "game," and the organization expects only from non-managerial employees to take more responsibilities with lower payment." As Participant #8 explained:

If management decides to treat employees fairly by giving reasonable salaries according to the responsibilities they assign to each one of us, then trust will increase between managers and employees. The HR department sent an email to everyone announcing 25%–30% salary reduction, which was applied as of two months ago. In other words, they announced it now, which is June, but they will deduct from our salaries as from April. Do you consider this fair? Do they expect us to trust them? And the answer is no, we will not trust them and it is really very sad that management does not understand that trust between management and employees is important to accomplish our organization's goals, and enhance team effectiveness during times of change.

Additionally, Participant #7 explained that team building can help maximize productivity, profitability, and customer service.

Job dissatisfaction

Five out of eight participants (62.5 percent) believed that when employees' perceptions of fairness on rewards and responsibilities that have been assigned since the MASC are considered to be fair, employees could experience job satisfaction. Participant #3 explained:

Fair rewards are usually accompanied by job satisfaction. Our organization didn't treat us fairly in reward and we have also undertaken more responsibilities since change. Because I am dissatisfied with the current working environment and with my work, I know that my job performance is decreased and my commitment too. Instead of the organization trying to improve the conditions of the workplace environment, offer more flexible work arrangements, and encourage employees to get more involved in their responsibilities, they announced via email the cutoffs in salaries and they also assigned us with new responsibilities with a lower salary.

Participant #7 asserted that they are not satisfied with their job because management did not do anything to satisfy employees' demands or even listen to their suggestions. "Employees expect from their employers to make them satisfied, communicate with them, and management has an obligation to do this, especially in times of strategic changes" (Participant #2). According to Participant #4:

Our organization is underpaying us and they assign new responsibilities that need more time since the changes. The stress of paying our bills, the schools of our children and other expenses with limited income make us feel dissatisfied with our jobs. This is unfair, to work more hours for less salary with more responsibilities. Sometimes I feel that I want to perform more in my job duties because I like my work, but I can't function when I know that I am underpaid. I experience boredom in the workplace and I have no incentives to be more productive.

Participant #6 stated that currently there is a lot of work pressure in the organization, which is a prime reason for job dissatisfaction — "Since our salary reduction, employees are asked to complete as many tasks as possible within a given time and this creates a huge work pressure on the employees." It's unfair that the organization, since the MASC, promoted some employees and increased their salaries; this causes job dissatisfaction (Participant #3; Participant #5).

FINDINGS FOR INTERVIEW QUESTION #4

Participants' responses to interview question #4, do you believe you have been treated with dignity and respect during this period of strategic change in the organization, revealed four emergent themes. These covered reduced withdrawal behaviors, improved job performance, working relationships, and communication. The following is an overview of participants' perspectives regarding these themes.

Reduced withdrawal behaviors

Six out of eight participants (75 percent) believed that when employees are treated with dignity and respect during strategic change in the workplace this could reduce withdrawal behaviors. "Employees expect fair, honest, and truthful treatments from the organization especially in times of strategic changes" (Participant #4). "Employees who perceive fair treatments and that the management treats them with dignity and respect are more likely to evidence positive actions like reduced withdrawal behaviors and willingness to work together with management to successfully implement the change" (Participant #1). As Participant #2 explained:

> I believe that I have been treated with dignity and respect from my manager during this period of strategic change, but my attitude changed negatively because I consider unfair the salary cut. There are a lot of factors that I think employees should examine before they make a final decision if they want to adopt a negative behavior in the organization. Management had to provide us with more information of what is really going on here and explain to us any decisions made. Every day we have new decisions, and if my manager was providing us with feedback on the situation we are experiencing, then my behavior towards the organization would change day by day to a positive one. I know that my manager, however, is trying to protect us, this person is also under big pressure from top management to follow what they are being instructed to do.

One participant believed that employers should have provided a more friendly and pleasant environment that supports teamwork to achieve goals in times of change (Participant #6). However, Participant #8 explained that

> Management could have provided us with feedback of this change before, during, and after the decision has been made from top management. I have been treated with dignity and respect, and this is one of the reasons that I try not to change my behavior towards my colleagues and towards the organization. Management must consider having open dialogue with employees because this will help to reduce any negative withdrawal behaviors we currently have in the workplace.

Participant #5 stated that, "Management did not treat employees with dignity and respect because of the fact that they did not show much concern for the treatment they received from top management, and the adequacy with which formal decision-making procedures are explained." Participant #6 added that, "Based on the continuation of unfair treatment from management, I'm more likely now to adopt negative actions in my behavior that in the end will result in my unwillingness to work together with my department to achieve organizational goals."

Improved job performance

Four out of eight participants (50 percent) believed that employees should be treated with dignity and respect during strategic change in the workplace in order to improve job performance. As Participant #7 explained:

> I am not satisfied with the way management treated me during strategic change. My manager's behavior was not honest and sometimes this person showed that they don't respect me because I did not get any answers or explanations to my questions. I cannot trust my manager, and if I don't trust this person then I will not be willing to cooperate with them in the workplace. I do not feel secure anymore and I'm not satisfied with my job. I was expecting my manager to be more honest with me.

In times of change, quality is under risk, job performance is at risk of decreasing, and management should treat employees with dignity and respect (Participant #1; Participant #5). Participant #6 stated that:

> There are some managers from some departments that are doing their best to keep employees informed of the changes taking place in the organization, promoting transparency; but my manager does not communicate any decision, that leads to low productivity and interest towards the organization.

Participant #1 asserted that:

> The manager is not willing to listen to our complaints or problems that we have in the department, and never apologizes even if they have made a mistake. I believe this is unfair, because we have the right to be aware about the current situation of our organization and what the organization is going through during this change. Personally, I'm more dissatisfied with my manager instead of top management because this is the person I see every day and the one providing me with information about the changes. If the business relationship with

my manager was a successful one, then I would be more productive and happy with my job.

Working relationships

Three out of eight participants (37.5 percent) believed that employees should be treated with dignity and respect during strategic change in the workplace in order to build a teamwork spirit and work closely with their colleagues to develop a positive attitude. One participant asserted that, "When employees are treated with dignity and respect during changes in an organization, trust can be developed between managers and employees, and employees are willing to work closer with their colleagues and be more effective in their tasks" (Participant #2). Participant #8 noted:

> *Working relationships can be encouraged when managers prove to employees that they are willing to work together to achieve the organization's goals. What we expect from them (managers) as employees is to avoid any negative thought and criticisms inside the organization and be less judgmental and more accepting of others. Because of all these changes that are taking place in the organization lately, managers are not direct with us, and they do not try to develop friendships with co-workers as they did before. They keep a distance from us, and we see that they set boundaries, and sometimes are rude to us. This behavior does not encourage us to work closer with them and try to develop a positive relationship in the workplace.*

According to Participant #5:

> *Because of the change there are a lot of negative situations that arise not only with clients but between our managers too. If they don't communicate with us and try to approach us in a friendly way, then we can't work together with them to resolve the different problems, but we make the problem bigger, which maybe we will never find a solution for.*

Participant #2 noted:

> *Employees should work together to develop a plan of action to resolve problems and present it to their managers to see how they can work together for a better solution.*

Communication

Six out of eight participants (75 percent) believed that employees should be treated with dignity and respect during strategic change in the organization in order to enhance communications with managers and employees so as to maximize service quality and internal communication. Participant #1 stated:

> Communication is a very important factor, and managers should focus on developing clear communication channels with employees. During times of change managers must communicate by opening up about what is happening with the organization, and communicate honestly and openly with employees. If communication is not present, then rumors will arise, like in our organization, and no one can stop them. But, when communication is effective during change, then employees and managers can work together to stop rumors.

There are two or three managers in the organization that understand the power of effective communication, and they implement it (Participant #6; Participant #8). According to Participant #8, "Some managers use effective communication as a foundation for improving relationships between internal employees or the different departments." Participant #3 noted, "Communication helps in building trust and impacting bottom line results especially in times of crises and in times of huge changes." Participant #5 asserted:

> Managers must treat employees with respect and honesty and listen carefully to our problems or suggestions. We need to feel we are a part of this change, and most of us are willing to work together with the management and find solutions. If we manage as an organization to achieve this, then we can avoid any misunderstandings between us, be open and honest about our feelings, and work together towards the organization's goals. If managers try to look at things from our own perspective, they will recognize the need for closer cooperation to reach common goals, because we are all in the same boat. If the boat sinks, everyone who is inside the boat will not be alive the next day. Feedback is also important, which is not very successful in our organization for a long time now.

According to Participant #2, "When managers keep active the communication between employees and the management they can easily identify attitudes and behaviors towards organizational changes and assess how well employees understand them." Participant #1 believed that:

> When employees feel unsure about the change plans, managers can provide them with feedback and this helps to improve the business and the way management manages and communicates change, but when communication is not effective then the company's goals will be hardly achieved in times of change.

FINDINGS FOR INTERVIEW QUESTION #7

Participant responses to interview question #7, do you feel that some of your peers have benefited more from the MASC than you have, revealed important insights into three emergent themes. These were job performance, behavior, and commitment. The following is a summary overview of participants' perspectives regarding these themes.

Job performance

Three out of eight participants (37.5 percent) believed that some of their peers have benefited more from the MASC than they have, and that this has had an effect on their job performance. Participant #3 explained:

> What happens now in the organization can't be explained because management proceeded with some promotions that are unfair. I believe that my performance was not rated fairly by management and my manager promoted another employee to a position that I had all the qualifications, skills, and experience to fulfill. I do not consider the evaluation to be fair, and I'm wondering if management's judgment was correct to promote an employee with below average experience to a position that requires at least six years' of experience. I am expecting from management to promote and act on fair decisions, because without being fair then I can't perform effectively in my job. Believe me, this sense of unfairness I'm going through for the past eight months creates a lot of stress for me and negative feelings. I can't function in the organization like before.

Alternatively, Participant #7 stated that:

> The organization does not follow certain procedures in the way benefits and promotions are distributed and this is why some of the employees

have benefited more from this change, and will be benefited more in the future if management continues to act like now.

Participant #1 believed that:

When employees perceive that the system is ineffective and unfair, employees are not willing to perform well in their work and adopt negative behavior towards their colleagues and towards management.

As Participant #6 stated:

After organizational change, some employees are working less hours with no salary decrease, and this is unfair. Management shouldn't expect that my performance would be the same as before.

Behavior

Four out of eight participants (50 percent) believed that none of their peers have benefited more from the MASC than they have, and this had an effect on their behavior towards their peers and in their workplace environment. When employees perceive that during times of change management treats all employees equally then they are more willing to work harder and adopt positive behaviors that will help the organization make the change more effectively (Participant #2; Participant #7). Participant #8 suggested that "Change affected everyone in the organization and I don't think that some of my peers have benefited more from this change. I feel that we became closer with our peers and we are more honest between us." Participant #1 believed that:

I consider that my organization is doing its best to remain socially responsible and this is the reason that I employ a positive attitude towards my colleagues, despite the fact that the change we are going through is very difficult. Some employees are working together and their behavior changed, because they know that if they do not cooperate with each other then this change will be more difficult for everyone. The organization must promote a positive work environment and promote fairness.

Participant #5 stated that when employees perceive a fair climate in the workplace and fair treatment from management towards employees in times of change, then employees interact positively and engage in positive behaviors.

Commitment

Five out of eight participants (62.5 percent) believed that when some employees benefit more than others from the MASC, this has an important effect on commitment. According to Participant #6:

> *I consider very important the fairness of management's decision-making policies and practices during change in the organization. If I notice that some of my peers have benefited more from this change than me, then the interest I have and the degree of commitment I show to my organization will definitely change. My organization is changing structure and didn't take into account how these actions will be perceived by employees.*

The importance of how the changes will take place and that all employees will be treated fairly are critical to the successful implementation of change and to the increased commitment on the part of the employees (Participant #3; Participant #5; Participant #8). Participant #4 asserted:

> *Strategic changes inevitably impacted employees to some degree in our organization and this has impacted their trust and motivation. I didn't feel that some of my peers have benefited more from the MASC than me to a large degree, but I noticed management trying to foster commitment among employees during these changes that are rapidly taking place. If commitment levels are not monitored on an ongoing basis and management does not give priority within the organization during change, then change will be implemented with difficulty because it will not have the support of the employees.*

As Participant #7 stated:

> *Change within media organizations is demanding, complex, and emotional for the employees and in the event that employees notice unfair actions from management, or that some employees have benefited more from them, there is a risk of adopting negative employee relationships amongst themselves and less commitment towards the organization.*

Employee commitment is associated with how the change process is managed by the organization and how fairly they treat employees in the workplace (Participant #2; Participant #6).

SUB-QUESTION 3

How can an organizational justice framework be used to explore employees' perceptions of the management of change within the context of strategic change?

To determine the third sub-question, participants were asked questions to identify whether management informed them with a thorough explanation of the MASC before enacting its agenda, and if yes, whether they believed the explanation was reasonable and accurate. Interview question #1 corresponded to this research sub-question and participant responses are detailed below.

FINDINGS FOR INTERVIEW QUESTION #1

Participants' responses to interview question #1, did management inform employees with a thorough explanation of the MASC before enacting its agenda, and if yes, did you believe the explanation was reasonable and accurate, revealed two emergent themes: communication and sharing of information, and trust. The following is an overview of participants' perspectives regarding these themes.

Communication and sharing of information

All eight participants (100 percent) believed that the role of management is very critical in an organization that is undergoing a strategic change, and that management must provide a communication strategy to share information with employees, supporting that in order for change to be sustained, management must try to maintain trust by encouraging meaningful dialogue with subordinate employees and maintain open contact with their managers. Participants expressed insightful opinions regarding why employees must have full support from organizational management in times of strategic change. Participant #5 asserted:

> *Organizational management must take an active role in such situations preparing their employees for the strategic change. In cases that change is not communicated successfully, and the management does not communicate to employees why and how this change will take place, employee resistance may increase, and the organization will not implement the change successfully. Management should communicate and work closely with employees, even have a communications team member to attend all senior management's meetings in order for that*

team member to be the contact for any one of the employees that will communicate to others the change initiatives. In our organization we still did not have any official communication of what is the current situation and what are the next steps of this change, what will happen with us. Internal communication and sharing of information from management can provide the best mechanisms that can make any strategic change to succeed and also may increase performance and productivity in the long term.

As participant #1 stated:

The role of human resources and communication is important in an organization that is undergoing change like ours, and managers have to explain clearly to employees what's going to happen, when, and how it will happen, and communication in our organization is like a drop in the ocean—not any communication at all. Managers should have had interaction with employees in order to develop trust, since verbal communication promotes the development of trust in the workplace.

Similarly, another participant supported that:

Management should be able to share any kind of information with their employees regarding how these changes are going to affect the things they are most worried about, like their benefits, pay, and job security, and that management's information is not successful in the media organization because it does not exist (Participant #7).

Participant #7 also noted that management does not provide effective communication within the organization with employees, and emphasized that the non-verbal part of communication is the most often overlooked part of the communication process from organizational management, resulting in miscommunication and unclear understanding by the employees when interacting with management, especially in times of change.

As Participant #4 stated:

We need to know what is expected from us from the management; they do not even send us an email or organize meetings to ensure a truly two-way communication. They just announce to us who will get fired from the organization and that some of us will have to work more hours without getting any overtime. There is an absence of communication from the management to us. I believe that the task of communication and sharing of information in times of change, like the one we have now in our organization, makes the difference not only for an organization, but also for its members. Communication is considered a factor that promotes clear guidelines and explanation where we are now, and how we will get to the new organization "state" after change, and this is an indication whether we will succeed or fail at the end of the day.

Another participant added that when management controls communication and what kind of information will be shared, monitoring feedback will be a good technique to catch rumors as they surface and trace more easily any gaps that have taken place between managers and employees (Participant #2). Participant #2 asserted:

As employees, we did recognize that the strategic change must take place in our organization. However, middle managers and the top management preferred not to involve or consider employees and entry-level staff in the implementation phase of this change. Management did not give us any explanation or information before enacting this change. In my opinion, regardless of how successful this planned organizational change may be, it will not be effectively implemented if the organization's employees are not aware of this change plan. The organization could easily avoid resistance or any fears, or even the strikes that are taking place if management had a stable communication line with employees. Confusion could also be minimized and employees' behaviors could change in favor of this change if they already knew what change was going to happen, and how this change was going to happen.

In addition, Participant #6 stated:

In cases that the organization keeps a "silent mode" strategy, like in our situation, instead of an open communication strategy with their employees in such difficult times, like the one we are going through now, it can cause fear and uncertainty among employees leading to a weaker and less productive organization. In our situation employees do not even have the opportunity to submit questions or address their concerns with their managers, because they feared that they will be fired if they dare to ask any kind of question regarding the changes that are taking place. Management didn't communicate to us the vision of change or even provide us with activities such as training courses or weekly meetings to see how we can fit into the change process, so that implementation could be successful.

Participant #8 asserted:

Communicating change is difficult, but if the organization offers practical steps in a communication strategy, then change can be successful if organizations employ managers who are leaders, and who have excellent communication skills. This is not our case of course. Managers do not behave in ways that are consistent with the vision they are promoting.

Following, Participant #3 noted that:

Management must communicate to their employees any key messages about the change and that these messages can help employees understand the reasons or forces of change, and that communication is an important step for employees to understand better the reasons why this change must take place.

Participant #3 added that there was a kind of information given to the employees but not something specific so that they could understand what was really going to happen, resulting in insecurity and unfavorable rumors within the organization. On the other hand, Participant #6 suggested that communication about change could help in changing old behaviors of employees that were against any kind of strategic change, and communication and sharing of information is the context within which change can successfully occur.

Trust

Six out of eight participants (75 percent) believed that when management provides information and is in direct contact with employees during the MASC, then trust towards to the organization can be maintained with employees. Effective communication is a fundamental factor in building trust between employees and managers, and contributes to the creation of a trustful environment, motivating employees to work even harder and be more productive, even in times of change (Participant #2; Participant #3; Participant #8). Participant #3 also stated that employee communications during times of strategic change may be evaluated, and management must assess perceptions of the current state of communication within the workplace. Management and non-managerial employees should work together to develop some kind of workshops to communicate the plan of change as well as offer methods of monitoring as to how these messages and plan of change are internalized throughout the organization. Participant #8 added that currently there is a lot of confusion and uncertainty in the organization and employees could more easily be willing to adapt to this change if they trusted management more.

In order for the change to succeed, management and non-managerial employees must communicate on an everyday basis because communication results in trust, and lends to implementing easier and more successfully this change (Participant #2).

Participant #1 asserted:

Communication from the management to employees in times of change is a key responsibility for organizations. Communication can help maintain or even create a culture in the organization in which trust can thrive. If we did have effective communication from management about these changes, we could build trust with our managers and support these changes too, but we did not. Developing trust within the workplace could help the change process we are undergoing now. The organization's staff needs to establish and maintain integrity and always be communicating the truth. If this was done in our organization employees could focus on shared goals, and not personal, and we could promote teamwork and trust each other.

Participant #6 stated:

Since management did not communicate the MASC at all, the trust that I used to have in the organization for the last seven years disappeared. I feel that I'm not secure now and I'm less productive. Because of the fact that management does not inform us of any changes, and they just proceed with announcements, this changed my behavior and my commitment towards the organization. Definitely, I can tell that my commitment has been reduced too towards the organization. But they all start from trust, when trust disappears, all the other negative factors like commitment, productivity, and employee engagement will not be my priority in the workplace like it was before.

In contrast, Participant #7 believed that management had provided them with some kind of information related to the current MASC that is taking place in the organization, by explaining why the change is critical during this period. "Communication in times of strategic change helps build trust among employees, and among management and employees. Building trust enhances productivity" (Participant #7). This participant concluded that their trust towards the organization remained the same as it was before, because the information communicated to them is considered to be adequate, and that management needs to understand how they can lose trust and what behaviors to avoid in the workplace, during strategic change. Participant #4 believed that the organization did not communicate any model for the change that is currently being implemented, and that top and middle management could be more committed to fostering communications between them and between non-managerial employees. As Participant #5 stated:

> I'm still wondering what change is going to take place in the organization. I think management does not know what are they doing, the messages they are communicating to us are not consistent with each other and this will lead to an overall failure of their change strategy. If they had a managerial team that would be responsible to communicate on behalf of the organization and note what the company's strategic objectives are to the employees, then this could reflect a clear understanding of the change.

Part C of the Interview Guide included additional data on psychological contract fulfillment and were based on a scale, The Psychological Contract Fulfillment Scale first developed and used by Henderson et al. (2008). The instructions to the participants were: "Please respond spontaneously with the first thoughts that come to mind upon hearing the following statements." This scale was developed as part of an investigation to highlight how Leader–Member Exchange (LMX) and psychological contract fulfillment processes work to shape the attitudes and behaviors of employees (Henderson et al., 2008: 1208).

RESPONSES FOR STATEMENT #1

Participant responses for statement #1, "My company has often broken promises made to me," varied substantially. A number of participants responded that the company didn't break any promises made to them (Participant #1; Participant #3; Participant #6). The organization tries to promise things that it can deliver to employees, because they know that in case they break promises to us they will have negative consequences in productivity (Participant #2; Participant #5). Alternatively, Participant #4 replied that the organization only once broke its promise but management offered a different solution to make the particular employee feel satisfied. Two participants responded that the organization didn't promise something that it couldn't implement (Participant #7; Participant #8).

RESPONSES FOR STATEMENT #2

Participant responses for statement #2, considering the promises my company has made to me, the company hasn't always lived up to its end of the bargain, were also varied. Two participants replied positively to this statement and they responded that the organization did not carry out what was promised initially until the end and they actually negotiated different things than those promised at the beginning, at the expense of the employees (Participant #5; Participant #6). Other participants replied that until now the organization has lived up to its end of the bargain, but they wondered whether this would be possible from now on with all these changes taking place (Participant #1; Participant #3; Participant #7; Participant #8). Two participants did not want to give their answer to this statement (Participant #2; Participant #4). Following, participant responses for statement #2 (reverse scored), "Considering the promises that I made to my company, I didn't always live up to my end of the bargain," all eight participants replied that for all the promises they made to the organization they always lived up to their end of the bargain.

RESPONSES FOR STATEMENT #3

Participant responses for statement #3, "My company has kept its promises to me," were contrasting. Two participants replied that this is true and even in times where the organization had some difficulties, they tried to keep the promises they made to employees (Participant #7; Participant #8). "This is so false, if the organization kept its promises to me I would be the happiest employee of the media organization," one of the participants replied (Participant #6). Other participants stated that "the company is trying to keep its promises; it's doing its best" (Participant #2; Participant #5). Participant #4 stated that, "The company keeps its promises only with the employees they like and who are closer with to management." Participant #1 agreed that for the past five years the company has kept its promises to employees, and now that it is in a difficult economic situation this person will show understanding even if the company does not keep to what it promised, as long as management offer employees a reasonable explanation. Participant #3 did not want to reply to this statement.

RESPONSES FOR STATEMENT #4

Participant responses for statement #4, "My company fulfills its obligations to me," were controversial. Five participants answered similarly, stating that their organization is trying to fulfill its obligations, although it is a very difficult period and that everything in the organization is undergoing change (Participant #1; Participant #2; Participant #5; Participant #7; Participant #8). Additionally, one participant stated that, "The organization from now on will not fulfill its obligations to the employees because many more big changes will follow" (Participant #3). Following, two other participants responded that the organization usually fulfills its obligations, and at least they try to do so considering the different difficulties that they have (Participant #4; Participant #6).

Thematic Analysis of the Textual Data Set

The researcher identified a number of overarching themes to be common in all questions. A thematic analysis was conducted to provide a more detailed and nuanced account of the group of themes emerging within the data. Themes were identified based on recurrence, repetition, and forcefulness during the interview process and aligned with the relevant theoretical and applied literature.

Emergent themes suggest that management holds a pivotal role in an organization that is undergoing a strategic change, and that managers must put in place a communication strategy to share information with employees, and encourage a dialogue between them for the sharing of information. Management must maintain a two-way communication dialogue with their employees on a daily basis. Another theme indicated that communication is also critical in building trust between employees and managers. This will contribute to establishing a trustful environment that prompts employees to work diligently and be more productive during times of organizational change. In addition, management could develop trust within the workplace with employees and this would help the change process to be effective in the long term with the support of employees.

With regard to whether employees were able to express their views and feelings during change, emergent themes pointed to employee organizational support, increase in performance, commitment, and employee turnover in cases where management allows employees to express their views and feelings.

Additional themes indicated that organizational commitment decreases when employees do not express their views and feelings during change, and employees' behaviors also change negatively towards the organization. Results further suggested that when employees are not able to express their views during the tremendous changes that are taking place in the work environment, they will report lower satisfaction with and commitment to management, lower trust, and decreased job security.

Other themes emerged from research findings that indicated that organizations should promote fairness in times of strategic change with regard to employee rewarding, considering the responsibilities assigned to employees in order to promote increased productivity, trust towards management, and job satisfaction. Results suggested that when the organization is more transparent regarding the processes by which decisions are made, this could lead to fair outcomes for employees. In addition, top management must consider employees' decisions, and that this could lead to organizational support for organizational change, as well as increased productivity.

Other themes coming to the fore from this study suggest that employees who perceive fair treatment and that management treats them with dignity and respect are more likely to evidence positive actions like reduced withdrawal behaviors and willingness to work together with management to implement the change successfully. Results further confirmed that when employees perceive that the system is ineffective and unfair, they are not willing to perform well in their work and adopt negative behavior towards their colleagues and towards management. Still other shared themes proposed that fair actions from management, employee relationships, and commitment are important factors to help the organization successfully implement strategic changes.

Different themes emerged from research results that align with the central research question of this study regarding how an organizational justice framework can be used to explore employees' perceptions of trust, fairness, and the management of change within the context of strategic change. For example, results suggested that employees expect fair, honest, and truthful treatment from the organization in times of strategic changes. In addition, research results showed that employees who perceive fair treatments and feel that management treats them with dignity and respect are more likely to evidence positive actions like reduced withdrawal behaviors and willingness to work together with management to successfully implement the change. Results further highlighted the significance of information sharing in the workplace in order for employees to continue having trust in management, since communication supports the information and willingness to interact with employees during times of uncertainty and ambiguity.

Evaluation of Findings

Research findings provided insights supported by the extant literature and that can be used to address the central question of this study. Findings suggested that management should treat employees fairly, and be honest and truthful especially during times of change. Findings further indicated that the role of management is very critical in an organization that is undergoing strategic change, and that management must provide effective communication and sharing of information with employees; by encouraging meaningful dialogue in the workplace, trust can be maintained. Two distinct elements make up interactional justice and are associated with how managers relay to employees the reasons for changes that need to be implemented as well as how they treat their employees. With regard to the first element, communication and justification for the change, it has been found "that employees are more likely to accept decisions, even unfavorable ones, when given an adequate and genuine reason" for them (Thornhill and Saunders, 2003: 71). This highlights the significant role of communication in managing change, as it has been proven with the results of this study. In particular, employees' perceptions of organizational justice can be positively influenced by developing effective strategies in relation to impending organizational changes, as well as focusing communication on the basis of the change and reasons behind its necessity.

A positive moderating influence can be realized regarding the perceptions of employees in relation to change implementation by management's application of fairness and sensitivity during the implementation of change. This element of interactional justice was also found by Thornhill and Saunders (2003) to be tied to communications. Organizational justice scholars investigated the impact of perceptions of justice on outcomes, including employee withdrawal behaviors (i.e., absenteeism, turnover), organizational commitment, job satisfaction, counterproductive work behavior (i.e., employee theft), organizational citizenship behavior, and job performance. Accordingly, research findings suggested that managers could help avert negative behaviors on the part of employees when their treatment is perceived to be fair and when management treats them with dignity and respect. As a result, employees will be willing to work together with management to implement the change.

Management must focus on perceived fairness since organizational justice is considered to have a positive impact on employee trust, where expectations are based on perceived motives and treatment. Employees who feel trust and have positive feelings regarding their treatment within the organizational context are willing to get involved in the change process, and can adopt a positive working relationship with their colleagues and their line managers. The present study's findings indicate that trust affects the quality of relationships between their peers and with their managers. Employees also noted the importance of information sharing in the workplace in order to continue having trust in management, since communication supports the information and willingness to interact with management during times of uncertainty and ambiguity.

Other findings indicated that employees would be willing to be committed when they experience fairness in the actions of and decisions by management, and they suggest that when employees feel committed in their workplace this helps the development of a good environment in the context of change. Findings further suggested that when employees perceive that the system is ineffective and unfair, they are not willing to perform well in their work and they adopt negative behaviors towards their colleagues and management. In addition, other results indicated that when employees perceive a fair climate in the workplace and fair treatment by management, they are more willing to interact positively and engage in positive behaviors.

Following the completion of eight interviews with participants and an analysis of the relevant transcriptions, findings emerging from this qualitative, multiple-case study are found to be in alignment with the theoretical concepts discussed in this body of work. One seminal theory that was used to support this study is Lewin's "*Three Step Model of Change*" (Lewin, 1958)—unfreezing, change, and refreezing. According to this model, change originates from two forces: those internally driven (from a person's own needs) and those imposed or induced by the environment. According to Lewin's concept of change, the unfreezing step involves getting people to accept the impending change. The change step has to do with convincing people to accept the new state, while the refreezing step intends to make permanent the new practices and behaviors once the implementation process has been concluded. The taxonomy of organizational justice theories by Greenberg (1987) was another theory that was used in this multiple-case study. Organizational justice theory is based on perceptions by employees, in any kind of organization, that they are being treated in a fair and just manner by their organization. The behaviors of employees in the workplace with regard to justice evolved into an area of study following the increasing importance attributed to the concept of justice.

In examining interpersonal trust, which is important for the motivation of workers to self-organize, research has shown that where trust is present it can promote a critical mass of trust-related behaviors, such as cooperation needed to create higher-unit trustworthiness. In this respect, Rousseau et al.'s (1998) trust theory was used as a supporting theory for this case study. By focusing on the dynamics of interpersonal trust-building in the workplace environment, trust theory indicates that the ability to demonstrate trust in times of change requires managers to engage their employees. Another theory used to support this study is that of Saunders and Thornhill (2003), which states that any influential factors on employees' perceptions of interpersonal justice are critical for building trust in the organization.

In addition, another theory that was used to support this study is Folger and Cropanzano's (1998) theory on fairness. Fairness theory does not reflect on the impact of procedures on fairness outcomes, and offers little in the way of outlining determinants of responses to unfair treatment by leadership towards subordinates in the workplace. However, the exploration of how justice evaluations are made in the workplace provides a framework for an organization on how to guide future behaviors.

This study was conducted to advance knowledge about how an organizational justice framework can be used to explore employees' perceptions of trust, fairness, and the management of change during a period of strategic change in a privately-owned media organization based in Cyprus. The results that follow are provided to describe how the theoretical literature used in this study compares or contrasts with actual research findings from participants' responses to interview questions. A comparative analysis is provided to describe how research findings contribute to the body of knowledge about employees' perceptions of trust, fairness, and the management of change in an organization undergoing change, using an organizational justice framework.

EVALUATION OF FINDINGS FOR INTERVIEW QUESTION #1

Did management inform employees with a thorough explanation of the MASC before enacting its agenda? If yes, did you believe the explanation was reasonable and accurate?

Study findings suggested that management should provide communication strategies and share information with employees, supporting that in order for change to be sustained management must maintain trust by encouraging meaningful dialogue with employees and have full support from them in times of strategic change. Other research results indicated that communication is considered a factor that promotes clear guidelines for and explanation to employees where the organization is at now, and how it will get to the new organizational "state" after change.

Employees will be willing to support organizational change when management monitors feedback to catch rumors, as participants said, that surface and carefully trace any communication gaps that may take place between managers and employees. Lewin's (1951) *"Three Step Model of Change"* —unfreezing, change, and refreezing—provides an outline that assists organizations to visualize, plan, and manage each of the stages of change, with communication being key to this model. In comparison with study findings, Lewin's model of change suggests that management should remain open and honest with feedback to staff and continue to build cohesiveness among the groups affected.

EVALUATION OF FINDINGS FOR INTERVIEW QUESTION #2

Have you been able to express your views and feelings during the MASC?

Study findings suggested that employees' perceptions and feelings should be considered by management and that employees have to be able to express their opinions and ideas about change. Other research results indicated that employees should express their views and feelings during change in order to be heard and have their views noted on the organization's decisions as to whether they are fair or not, regardless of the outcome. Folger and Cropanzano's (1998) theory on procedural justice suggests that procedural justice emphasizes the perceived fairness of how the amount of punishment or reward is determined; the way in which outcomes are determined possibly holds greater weight than the final outcome. Accordingly, study results are consistent with Folger and Cropanzano's theory that employees would exhibit greater loyalty and trust in the organization and be willing to work for their organization's best interest if they perceive that a decision-making process is fair.

EVALUATION OF FINDINGS FOR INTERVIEW QUESTION #3

How fair has your organization been in rewarding you when you consider the responsibilities you have been assigned since the MASC?

Research findings suggested that employees should perceive that the new responsibilities assigned to them and the level of pay they receive are considered to be fair, otherwise productivity will decrease. Other findings indicated that fair rewards should be accompanied by job satisfaction. Study findings are consistent with Saunders and Thornhill's (2004) organizational justice theory, which indicates that distributive justice integrates fairness perceptions regarding organizational outcomes. Results provide further understanding of Saunders and Thornhill's (2004) theory, which suggests that when employees feel that there is distributive justice in the workplace, they are more likely to feel more trusting towards management; this is linked with job satisfaction, commitment, and lower turnover intentions.

EVALUATION OF FINDINGS FOR INTERVIEW QUESTION #4

Do you believe you have been treated with dignity and respect during this period of strategic change in the organization?

Research results suggest that employees should expect fair, honest, and truthful treatment by management in times of change because then they are more likely to adopt positive actions, like reduced withdrawal behaviors and willingness to work together with management to successfully implement change. Findings further suggest that managers should strengthen relations with employees in times of change to build a teamwork spirit, and work closely with them and be more effective in their tasks. In addition, research findings indicated that managers should focus on the development of clear communication channels with employees, and communicate honestly and openly with them. Interactional justice theory refers to how adequately the information being communicated is used to explain how decisions are made and how thoroughly accounts of these decisions are provided. Interactional justice theory focuses on the quality of interpersonal treatment an employee receives during the implementation of organizational procedures, which is consistent with study findings.

EVALUATION OF FINDINGS FOR INTERVIEW QUESTION #5

Since the enactment of the MASC how do you perceive that your attitude towards your organization has been affected?

Research results indicated that management should promote communication and sharing of information in the workplace in order for employees to build trust with management. Further findings suggested that trust affects the quality of relationships, and that management should make good-faith efforts and behave with honesty in relation to employees. Other findings indicated that employees who feel trust can focus on positive aspects when talking about their reactions to organizational change and be more enthusiastic in promoting positive working relationships with their colleagues and their line managers. Study findings are consistent with organizational trust theory, which is an important factor that can promote successful business practices, within and between organizations. When individuals are interactively involved in trust-building, action and trust can mutually reinforce each other, as is also suggested in this study's findings.

EVALUATION OF FINDINGS FOR INTERVIEW QUESTION #6

Since the enactment of the MASC how do you perceive that your attitude towards your peers has been affected?

Research results indicated that a thankful and positive attitude on the part of employees towards their peers promotes trust, and a positive working environment that helps to reinforce specific behaviors. Further findings suggested that behaviors that build trust are linked to strategic business outcomes such as improved performance in the organization and successful teamwork in times of change. Organizational trust theory indicates that trust is at the core of all interpersonal relationships, holding people together and offering individuals a sense of security. The trust construct is a key element promoting effective communication as well as teamwork between co-workers, and between employees and managers. Communication between employees during organizational changes helps to avoid negative attitudes and behaviors in the workplace, which is consistent with this study's findings.

EVALUATION OF FINDINGS FOR INTERVIEW QUESTION #7

Do you feel that some of your peers have benefited more from the MASC than you have?

Key research findings indicated that in order for employees to be willing and work hard, management should adopt positive behaviors and be more committed to the organization. Other findings suggested that when employees perceive that the system is ineffective and unfair, they are not willing to perform well in their work and, as a result, they adopt negative behavior towards their colleagues and towards management. Perceptions of distrust and unfairness can lead to resistance and negative behaviors directed at organizations and management during change, which is consistent with this study's findings.

Following, research findings are consistent with Folger and Cropanzano's (1998) theory of fairness, which indicates that fairness in organizations affects behaviors and results in the workplace; the exploration of how justice evaluations are made in the workplace provides a framework for organizations on how to guide future behaviors.

Responses from The Psychological Contract Fulfillment Scale and their evaluation in terms of implications for organizations undergoing strategic change are as follows:

EVALUATION OF FINDINGS FOR STATEMENT #1

Please respond spontaneously with the first thoughts that come to mind upon hearing the statement: "(My company) has often broken its promises to me." Research results indicate that organizations must endeavor to fulfill promises made to employees, as failure to do so will likely have negative consequences regarding productivity. However, if circumstances necessitate going back on a promise, management should offer another solution so as to make employees feel satisfied.

EVALUATION OF FINDINGS FOR STATEMENT #2

Please respond spontaneously with the first thoughts that come to mind upon hearing the statement: "Considering the promises my company has made to me, the company hasn't always lived up to its end of the bargain." Based on the study's results, when an organization makes good on what was initially promised rather than negotiating different aspects of the new work environment and responsibilities assigned to employees, as well as rewards, employees will be inclined to perceive fair treatment or that they are being treated with dignity and respect by management. In such cases, employees will assume more positive behaviors such as reduced withdrawal and a willingness to work with management to successfully implement changes. Also, to reduce uncertainty, management should indicate whether going forward they will be able to keep fulfilling promises made as changes continue to take place. It follows that this will also prompt employees to fulfill the promises that they have made to their company.

EVALUATION OF FINDINGS FOR STATEMENT #3

Please respond spontaneously with the first thoughts that come to mind upon hearing the statement: "My company has kept its promises to me." Study results indicate that employees may be inclined to view in a favorable manner, efforts by their organization to keep their promises, even in times where the organization is experiencing difficulties. If promises are broken, employees should be provided with a reasonable explanation as to why. However, results strongly indicated that management should consider that employees will be much happier when promises made are kept. This will add to a more positive environment and increased productivity. Furthermore, management in organizations undergoing change need to be mindful of which promises are kept for which employees so as not to create a climate deemed as unfair by those who did not have their promises kept. In such instances, employees may feel that decisions are based on bias towards employees who are better liked or are closer to management.

EVALUATION OF FINDINGS FOR STATEMENT #4

Please respond spontaneously with the first thoughts that come to mind upon hearing the statement: "My company fulfills its obligations to me." The study's findings indicate that employees are able to discern when their organization is making an effort to fulfill its obligations during a difficult period of change. Additionally, employees will form opinions as to whether their organization will be able to continue fulfilling its obligations in light of impending changes.

Summary

The aim of this qualitative, embedded multiple-case study was to increase knowledge regarding employees' perceptions of trust, fairness, and the management of change during a period of strategic change in a privately-owned media organization based in Cyprus, using an organizational justice framework. This multiple-case study examined factors that could contribute to a richer understanding of employees' perceptions of trust, fairness, and the management of change using an organizational justice framework. It also sought to advance knowledge that could help organizational leadership recognize the significance of establishing mutual trust with their employees so they may successfully cooperate with management during times of strategic change. In addition, this multiple-case study investigated employees' perceptions of fairness towards organizations during strategic change, considered a critical factor for organizations during change, the results of which can be used to guide management in preventing destructive actions of employees who perceive they have been unfairly treated by their supervisors. Following, this multiple-case study examined the management of change within the organizational justice literature as a means of helping organizations improve on human resources management processes and procedures, including those relevant to change, the way they function, and formal and informal rules protecting employees' rights as well as the organizational culture.

The researcher interviewed eight non-managerial employees who had at least three years of work experience in the media organization and who were active in sales or carrying out responsibilities as technicians or cameramen. Of the eight participants, four worked in sales positions, two were technicians, and two were cameramen. The purpose of this research was to examine how an organizational justice framework can be used to explore employees' perceptions of trust, fairness, and the management of change during a period of strategic change in a privately-owned media organization based in Cyprus.

Different methodologies were used in this study to establish triangulation and validate participants' intended meanings. The researcher digitally recorded and then transcribed interview sessions with the eight participants for an analysis aimed at assessing patterns as well as themes that emerged from each interview. During the interview sessions, handwritten notes were kept to capture key comments and important responses offered by participants. By corroborating content detailed in the transcriptions with field notes, and by providing participants with their transcriptions to check for discrepancies, the researcher was able to achieve triangulation. The results of this action confirmed that there were no discrepancies in the transcripts. Transcripts of the interview sessions were uploaded to NVivo software (Version 9) in order to assign codes and nodes. Subsequently, the researcher used this aid to analyze frequent occurrences of words as well as results. A review of handwritten notes was carried out to corroborate themes in comparison to coded data.

Various themes emerged as a result of key findings that align with the extant literature. Study findings for the first interview question indicated that communication and sharing of information as well as trust are critical for giving a reasonable and accurate explanation to employees regarding strategic change on the part of management. Emergent themes for the second interview question covered organizational support, performance and employee turnover, organizational commitment, and behavioral change as approaches that employees are likely to adopt when they are able to express their views and feelings during times of change. Results for the third interview question revealed themes related to productivity, trust, and job dissatisfaction—factors that play a role regarding employees' feelings towards the organization in relation to fairness since the implementation of strategic changes. The fourth interview question brought forth emergent themes in relation to reduced withdrawal behaviors, improved job performance, working relationships, and communication as manifested by employees when they are treated with dignity and respect during strategic changes in the organization. Participant responses to the fifth interview question resulted in themes regarding trust, organizational relationships, and commitment as being the employee perceptions and the attitudes affected since the enactment of the strategic change. Emergent themes from the sixth interview question covered areas of teamwork, trust, and communication as important attitudes that employees could have towards their peers since the enactment of the MASC. The final interview question revealed job performance, behavior, and commitment as emergent themes regarding employee feelings related to whether some of their peers have benefited more than they have from the MASC.

Scholars of organizational change contend that change constitutes a natural component of the working lives of employees. An organizational justice framework offers a means for better understanding, within the context of strategic change, employees' perceptions of trust, fairness, and the management of change in an organization. Given that strategic change is an inevitable factor in the life cycle of modern organizations, the findings from this study contribute to a better understanding of how change in organizations can be successfully and more effectively implemented, as well as how to forecast employees' reactions so as to bring about the desired change.

Chapter 8
Implications

The problem addressed in this qualitative case study is how an organizational justice framework could address the need raised by scholars of organizational justice (for example, Colquitt and Greenberg, 2003; Mayer et al., 2007) for novel, conceptually derived accounts of non-managerial employee perspectives on organizational justice during periods of organizational change. The purpose of this qualitative study was to examine how an organizational justice framework can be used to explore employees' perceptions of trust, fairness, and the management of change during a period of strategic change in a privately-owned media organization based in Cyprus. A multiple-case study research design was used to satisfy the goal of this exploratory research and data were collected through multiple sources, including in-depth individual interviews, and SME review and reflection of the data collected. The researcher conducted eight in-depth, face-to-face interviews with employees from the media organization, four were from sales, two worked as technicians, and two worked as cameramen. For the purpose of this study, the researcher developed semi-structured interview questions, and the same questions were posed to each of the eight participants. Meaningful research was needed to increase knowledge about better understanding of employees' perceptions of trust, fairness, and the management of change, using an organizational justice framework within the media organization.

The qualitative case study method is appropriately used when researchers ask "how" or "why" questions regarding contemporary sets of events over which the investigator has minimal or no control. Case study researchers seek greater understanding of an issue and its complexity. As Eisenhardt and Graebner (2007) suggested, this design enables investigators to arrive at more generalized conclusions based on the totality of their specific observations. Since "how" and "why" questions were used to examine in-depth perceptions of selected participants from a media organization based in Cyprus, a multiple-case study design was used for this research. The current study employed purposeful selection of participants who were interviewed to generate responses. The strategy for selecting participants for a purposeful convenience employed a small group of homogeneous participants that provided an information-rich sample for the purpose of this study, from a media organization in the Nicosia area, Cyprus. The researcher's sampling strategies were aligned with the purpose of the study, resources available, questions asked, and constraints being faced. First, a pilot study was conducted as a basis for confirming the applicability and dependability of the research questions and data collection techniques of the research. Three participants were selected through purposive and snowball sampling, and pilot study participants had the same characteristics of subjects. The goal of the pilot study was to identify ambiguities, help to clarify the wording of questions, and allow early detection of necessary additions or omissions. Participants in the pilot study were not interviewed in the full study, and data for the pilot study was not included as part of the full research.

This study was designed to represent a sample of diverse individuals based on gender and work experience. Men and women between the ages of 25 and 55 volunteered to participate in this study. Each digitally recorded interview session with participants lasted approximately 40 to 60 minutes. Data gathered from recorded interview sessions were transcribed and coded in NVivo (Version 9) software. Unique terms that emerged from interviews were sorted into categories and analyzed to discover emergent themes and linkages.

Limitations were identified that could affect the perceived outcomes of this study. For instance, the fact that only one privately-owned media organization that is undergoing a strategic change in Cyprus was examined could have biased perceptions based on their explanations of perceptions of trust, fairness, and the management of change. Participants were asked to provide specific information about where they work, and may have biases about employers' competitive advantages or competitors, which could affect perspectives and perceptions. However, the methodology that was developed and tested during the study can also be used by other media organizations in Cyprus that are undergoing a strategic change to explore employees' perceptions of trust, fairness, and the management of change using an organizational justice framework. Another limitation for this study is that participants could have different perceptions that stem from cultural background, work experiences, educational level, and knowledge of employers' competitive positions in the workplace.

In addition, another identified limitation was that the study will not be repeated at a later time to compare results with initial findings. Changing economic conditions in the future could affect participants' perceptions of trust, fairness, and the management of change in an organization undergoing change. The researcher also recognizes that economic trends in the media environment in Cyprus, internally and externally, could influence study participants' perceptions regarding factors that affect their perceptions of trust, fairness, and the management of change. Following, another limitation was how statements, behaviors, and relationships with participants could influence research results. The researcher encouraged open communication with all participants and clarified the meaning of the research process and interview questions in order to support positive relations with the respondents.

High ethical standards were maintained in this research process by respecting participants' right to privacy and confidentiality. The identities of participants were not revealed in this study. All participants authorized informed consent forms prior to answering interview questions. Participants were informed about the purpose of the research, data collection, ethical standards, informed consent process, and opportunities to receive research results before conducting the interviews.

Participants in this study were encouraged to volunteer and express their perceptions, experiences, and comments. The participants felt confident that in-depth responses were held confidential and anonymous. Recorded interview sessions acknowledged participants by number classification rather than names. The only incentive offered to individuals for participating in this study was the opportunity to receive an electronic copy of the research results. To ensure academic integrity and maintain honesty with professional colleagues, the researcher presented truthful positions and statements regarding this research study and resulting outcomes.

The implications, recommendations, and conclusions of this study are provided to offer insights regarding the study's findings. The semi-structured interview questions used in this research are described. Interpretation is provided for key research question results. Recommendations are provided to describe opportunities for practice and future research opportunities that others may pursue to enhance knowledge of employees' perceptions of trust, fairness, and the management of change using an organizational justice framework, in a media organization undergoing strategic change. Conclusions are presented to summarize research findings. It is recommended that research continue to advance findings in this area.

Implications

The specific problem addressed in this qualitative case study is how an organizational justice framework could address the need raised by scholars of organizational justice (for example, Colquitt and Greenberg, 2003; Mayer et al., 2007) for novel, conceptually derived accounts of non-managerial employee perspectives on organizational justice during periods of organizational change. The purpose of this qualitative study was to examine how an organizational justice framework can be used to explore employees' perceptions of trust, fairness, and the management of change during a period of strategic change in a privately-owned media organization based in Cyprus. The findings and implications related to each research question and corresponding responses are discussed below.

RESEARCH QUESTION #1

> *How can an organizational justice framework be used to explore employees' perceptions of trust, fairness, and the management of change within the context of strategic change?*

Greenberg (1987) developed the taxonomy of organizational justice theories concerning justice and workplace perceptions of fairness. Additional studies were recommended to add to the existing organizational justice theories, illustrating how efforts to test theory-based applications can offer clearer insight into prevailing theories. Accordingly, the researcher found that employees' perceptions about trust, fairness, and the management of change, as well as justice-related problems, are important factors for managers to consider and be aware of within their workplace. Ensuring this is important, an implication of this study is that employee perceptions about trust, fairness, and the management of change can guide management to prevent destructive actions on the part of employees who perceive they have been treated unfairly by their supervisors. Managers should be able to explain and categorize the feelings and views of employees regarding employee treatment in the workplace environment.

This study's findings indicate that the impact of employees' perceptions of organizational justice is associated with a variety of individual factors such as organizational commitment, organizational trust, organizational change, managers' communication of organizational change to employees, and job satisfaction. Lind and van den Bos (2002) indicated that one of the most fruitful areas of research is the examination of organizational justice effects after the implementation of organizational change. Justice perceptions and assessments of trust could act as predictors of attitudes and behaviors on the part of the employee in the workplace. When employees feel that there is a lack of justice, then they are more likely to have thoughts of leaving the organization, employ negative attitudes, and resist organizational change.

RESEARCH QUESTION #2

How can an organizational justice framework be used to explore employees' perceptions of trust within the context of strategic change?

Factors that may influence employees' perceptions of interpersonal justice and the effect they have on building trust in the organization were studied by Saunders and Thornhill (2004). On the basis of their findings, the authors opined that trust reduces uncertainty, in addition to complexity, as unfavorable expectations are removed and favorable expectations are seen as certain. In addition, Rousseau et al. (1998) examined interpersonal trust and its importance in motivating workers to self-organize. Moreover, Rousseau et al. suggested that where trust is present, it can promote a critical mass of trust-related behaviors, such as cooperation needed to create higher-unit trustworthiness. This study's results imply that employees' overall feelings of trust are likely to be more significant when they feel it to exist, at both an organizational and personal level, and that organizational trust may be a prerequisite to establishing organizational effectiveness. Other findings from the current study suggest that trustable behavior between supervisors and employees can have a positive effect on organizational results and have an influence on employees' attitudes, such as performance, and efficiency, toward their organizations, thus boosting productivity.

A further implication of this study is that when employees feel that management trusts them this could enhance their performance in the organization and their productivity. Workers' trust in management is more likely to improve performance in the organization under change. This study further solidified organizational justice as an important predictor of employee attitudes and behaviors.

RESEARCH QUESTION #3

How can an organizational justice framework be used to explore employees' perceptions of fairness within the context of strategic change?

An implication of the study is that employees' perceptions of fairness in the workplace could be associated with their cooperative work behaviors, organizational commitment, and job satisfaction. Workplace fairness is operationalized in accordance with whether employees in lower levels feel their organizations' procedures (e.g., performance evaluation process) are fair or not. Employees expect managers to employ fair actions during times of strategic change.

A further implication is that through its impact on attitudes, organizational justice may affect the performance of employees, or distrust towards the organization. During a period of change managers should communicate and inform employees about the "why," "how," and "what next," offering clarification and compelling justification for the change, as well as providing a greater sense of control over it. In times of change, organizations need to be especially attentive to employees' perceptions of fairness of proposed organizational outcomes so that the organizational change can be successful. Employees are more likely to notice the relative distribution of salaries and benefits in the organizational context during change, when organizations allocate outcomes in agreement with implied norms for allocation, such as equality or equity. A further implication of these results is that among the three dimensions of organizational justice, distributive justice was found to be the strongest construct, being associated with trust in management, job satisfaction, and lower turnover intentions.

A study analyzing how managers' decisions can influence subordinates' perceptions of justice in organizational life was conducted by Folger and Cropanzano (1998). Here, the authors suggested that fairness does not reflect on the impact of procedures on fairness outcomes, and offers little in the way of outlining determinants of responses to unfair treatment on the part of leadership towards subordinates in the workplace. An implication of this study, based on its results, is that employees form judgments about fair and unfair treatment by comparing their situations regarding treatment and outcomes with those of others. Findings suggest that employees who perceive their workplace as a just and fair one are more likely to enjoy job satisfaction and less likely to leave as they have a higher sense of commitment to their job.

RESEARCH QUESTION #4

How can an organizational justice framework be used to explore employees' perceptions of the management of change within the context of strategic change?

Organizational justice can act as an indicator for the effective implementation of a change initiative, and be used as a contingency framework for understanding employees' perceptions of trust, fairness, and the management of change during strategic change, thus enabling effective action in the organizational environment, as called for by various researchers. The most controversial organized approach to change is regarded as that created by Kurt Lewin in 1958. Lewin (1958) developed the *"Three Step Model of Change"*—unfreezing, change, and refreezing—which was an outcome of his earlier seminal contributions to areas such as action research, field force theory, and group dynamics. Current research findings suggest that management should engage in communications with employees to define and explain the reasons why organizational change is required. Study findings indicate that the information communicated needs to be monitored and feedback solicited. Conversely, if the communication efforts from management to employees are weak, employees will view the change in a negative fashion, as per this study's findings.

Neves and Caetano (2006) and Saunders and Thornhill (2003, 2011) studied the role of supervisory trust, justice perceptions, and commitment in implementing organizational changes. Another implication of this study is that trust affects the quality of relationships, and management should make good-faith efforts and behave with honesty towards employees. In addition, this study's findings indicate that employees who feel trust can focus on positive aspects when talking about their reactions to organizational change and be more enthusiastic about promoting positive working relationships with their colleagues and their line managers.

Management should treat employees with politeness, dignity, and respect, since such treatment may be linked with job satisfaction, withdrawal behavior, commitment to the organization, and performance. Management that fails to treat employees fairly could influence employees' feelings of distrust in the workplace during change. Management should seriously consider the implications of interactional justice in times of strategic change, since employees who believe they are fully informed about the strategic change would feel a higher sense of affiliation and trust towards the organization.

Employees are likely to experience uncertainty in their everyday life because of strategic changes in their organization, which affects their justice judgments and whether or not they can trust their managers. One of the goals of this study was to provide managers with a framework to use to improve the effective implementation of organizational change. Organizational justice serves as such a framework. Employees who are treated in a just manner by management in times of change are more committed and consider fairness as an important trust element in order to form their perceptions of trust. Managers could gain knowledge that perceptions of distrust and unfairness can lead to resistance and negative behaviors directed at organizations and management during change.

Finally, results from research findings suggest other implications for organizations and employees regarding psychological contract violation. Management should not break its promises in relation to remuneration or job description because this could have an important influence on employees' behaviors and attitudes. Employees could react in a negative manner on the basis of the perceived violation of psychological contract. Managers who do not realize that organizational change may cause employees to re-interpret their psychological contracts are typically less prepared to deal with any implications for future commitment and contribution to the organization on behalf of employees. Management should realize the positive impact of adhering to organizational justice principles in the workplace in times of change vis-à-vis the employee–organization relationship.

Results in Relation to Purpose, Significance, and Existing Literature

The following describes how findings of the research questions align with the research purpose and compare or contrast with the literature review.

RESEARCH QUESTION #1

> *How can an organizational justice framework be used to explore employees' perceptions of trust, fairness, and the management of change within the context of strategic change?*

Research findings offer unique insights that management should consider regarding the information and explanation that they should give to employees, reasonable and accurate, before enacting the organizational agenda for strategic change. Findings indicate that management should build communications channels inside the organization between employees, in order to share information with employees. Study results further indicate that effective communication is a fundamental factor in building trust between employees and managers, and contributes to the creation of a trustful environment between managers and employees. Study findings suggest that if employees understand why actions are taken, what is expected, and how the change will lead through the steps toward the vision, they are more likely to support the organization on its strategic change journey. When employees do not have information during change, they are more likely to resist or even sabotage organizational change efforts that appear to threaten their job stability and security. Further findings indicate that when employees perceive that there are closed communication channels between management and employees on issues of strategic change that directly affect their job security, salary, and benefits, they are left with feelings of anger and resentment towards the employer. Moreover, employees report that when finding themselves in this situation their negative feelings from work affect their personal life, leading to irritability, anxiety, and mild depression. In addition, employees indicate that management should encourage them to talk about their feelings and what they believe they will lose as a result of change, in order to establish mutual trust with management.

Lewin's (1951) unfreezing, change, and refreezing model ascertained that during the transition phase an organization aims to shift or change employees' behaviors in the organization in which the changes are taking place. The author supported that through continual communication people will feel more involved and connected to the process of change. Researchers concluded that perceptions of trust and fairness could influence employees' reactions and attitudes towards a change initiative. Other researchers support that the social relationship between employees and supervisors during change can build trust and is a critical factor for successful organizational changes. Following, Neves and Caetano (2006) suggested that the process of informing employees and sharing of information about the proposed change is a very important factor in order to understand and support the change.

Research findings clearly suggest communication and sharing of information between management and employees, and the objectives of the change management effort. Further, research findings indicate that employees need to understand how these changes will affect them personally, suggesting that trust develops through communication and takes up more time than any other activity. Greenberg (1993) ascertained that interactional justice is more concerned with the feedback and concerns of employees in the organization, with knowledge and information being provided in cases where employees express related concerns, as well as explanations and information given to employees by management that provide detail on fairness procedures and outcome distribution. Cropanzano et al. (2002) and Rupp and Cropanzano (2002) indicated that in comparison with procedural justice, interactional justice primarily has impact on individual-level outcomes while procedural justice impacts organization-level outcomes. Judgments of interactional justice are influenced by factors such as honesty, ethical appropriateness, respect for rights and privacy, politeness, courtesy, keeping promises, and safeguarding secrets. On the other hand, high levels of interactional justice have been found to mitigate unfavorable attitudinal and behavioral reactions to perceived inequities. Interactional justice theory focuses on the quality of interpersonal treatment an employee receives during the implementation of organizational procedures, which is consistent with study findings.

Study findings indicate that employees should be able to express their views and feelings during strategic change in order to support the organization in the change initiative and increase their performance and turnover. Other study findings indicate other positive outcomes, such as tighter organizational commitment and positive behavioral change. Further research results suggest that employees should express their feelings and views during change in order to be heard and have their views taken into account on organization's decisions if they are fair or not, regardless of the outcome. Other findings indicate that employees' perceptions of procedural justice could promote acceptance of outcomes even when the outcomes are unfavorable. In line with this view, additional study findings ascertain that the way in which managers treat employees can lead to increased perceptions of organizational support and performance, and enhance trustworthiness and commitment of a manager.

Research results align with findings from different authors. Seminal authors Saunders and Thornhill (2003) asserted that procedural justice is seen as the perceived fairness of processes employed in the distribution of responsibilities, compensation, and rewards. Ambrose and Schminke (2009) posited that decision control is considered an important contributor to perceptions of justice in the workplace. Other authors indicated that through its impact on attitudes, procedural justice may affect the performance and actions of employees. Folger and Cropanzano (1998) suggested that employees would exhibit greater loyalty and trust in the organization and be willing to work for their organization's best interest if they perceive that a decision-making process is fair. Other researchers indicated that employees' perceptions of procedural justice are linked to their satisfaction with supervisors and commitment to the organization, a conclusion aligned with the results of this study.

Research findings suggest that the impact of employees' perceptions on outcomes such as work productivity, job performance, and organizational citizenship behavior are strongly linked with organizational justice in the workplace. According to other scholars, employees' perceptions of organizational justice are likely associated with other individual factors such as organizational commitment, organizational trust, and organizational change. Since perceptions of justice "are, in part considered to be influenced by outcomes one receives from the organization" (Cohen-Charash and Spector, 2001: 282), employees' justice perceptions can be moderated by events, such as strategic change in the workplace, based on exchanges perceived as fair on the part of management.

RESEARCH QUESTION #2

How can an organizational justice framework be used to explore employees' perceptions of trust within the context of strategic change?

Other results suggest that employees' attitudes towards their organization are affected in relation to organizational trust and organizational relationships. Research results indicate that management should promote communication and sharing of information in the workplace in order for employees to build trust with management and promote organizational relationships. Further findings suggest that trust is a critical factor in promoting effective communication and commitment towards the organization. Other findings indicate that employee commitment in times of change is positively related to job satisfaction, job performance, and motivation; the criterion for successful change includes an assessment of organizational trust, and efficient organizational change is highly reliant upon the existence of organizational and interpersonal trust in the workplace environment. Moreover, employees report that organizational management must understand how to assess a situation to determine the missing component in the trust process between management and supervisors. Other findings indicate that trust influences change and the procedure in which management integrates the change into the organization. The study's findings reveal that commitment is considered an important factor in organizational functioning and accounts for numerous employee-related attitudes and behaviors. Similar concepts are described in the literature review.

Organizational trust offers many important benefits for organizations and their employees. Employees who receive fair treatment from their supervisors, but not from their co-workers, have different justice perceptions about each party. Gilstrap and Collins (2012) ascertain that organizational trust is a very important factor for effective day-to-day functioning of the organization as indicated in this study's findings. Kim, Kim, and Kim (2008) suggest that when fairness is believed to be present in an organization, it is possible for trust to develop. Saunders and Thornhill (2004) posited that organizational trust can reduce complexity in organizational relationships, and promote justice and fairness in the organization. Similar concepts described in the literature review as such focus on how organizational justice in the workplace can influence organizational trust and support. Rousseau et al. (1998) indicated that when individuals employ a mutually trusting relationship, action and trust will reinforce each other.

Study findings are similar to concepts described by Rousseau et al. (1998) who asserted that organizational trust is at the core of all interpersonal relationships holding people together and offering individuals a sense of security. Colquitt and Rodell (2011) ascertained that organizational trust promotes effective communication as well as team work between co-workers, and between employees and managers. Justice and trust have been shown to be critical elements for organizational relationships and for understanding processes in organizational communication and between subordinate employees.

Trust affects the quality of relationships, communication, work, and every effort in the organization. Saunders and Thornhill (2004) asserted that individual behaviors are seen as part of trust-building, helping individuals to learn about the intentions of others on the basis of observation and interpretation, and to make judgments about trustworthiness and act upon these judgments. Saekoo (2011) indicated that organizational trust is considered an important ingredient for successful workplace relationships and can motivate people to commit to their organizations. Employees showed more willingness to promote their functions and performance and be more efficient in increasing organizational productivity when there is a strong relationship between organizational justice and trust. Saunders (2011) posited that employees who feel trust in organizational management can focus on positive aspects when talking about their reactions to organizational change, and adopt an enthusiastic spirit to promote positive working relationships with their colleagues, as is also well indicated in this research study's findings. According to Jones and Skarlicki (2012), organizational members face uncertainty in their workplace, which affects their judgments and whether or not they can show trust in their managers. In order for organizational management to successfully manage uncertainty in the workplace, individuals try to anticipate how fairly they will be treated in the future.

RESEARCH QUESTION #3

How can an organizational justice framework be used to explore employees' perceptions of fairness within the context of strategic change?

Research findings suggest that organizations should promote fair treatment approaches in times of strategic change, since employees' perceptions of fairness are associated with important and positive organizational variables like job satisfaction, job performance, citizenship behaviors, and commitment to an organization, which correlates with the literature review. Seminal authors Cohen-Charash and Spector (2001), Colquitt, Conlon, Wesson, Porter, and Ng (2001), and more recently Garcia-Izquierdo, Moscoso, and Ramos-Villagrasa (2012) asserted that perceived justice is associated with positive organizational outcomes such as job satisfaction, job performance, citizenship behaviors, and commitment to an organization. Dierendonck and Jacobs (2012) indicated that fairness was also shown to be more important when large strategic changes were taking place in the organization. On the other hand, perceptions of distrust and unfairness can result in resistance and negative behaviors directed at organizations and management during strategic changes.

Seminal authors Folger and Cropanzano (1998) and Greenberg (1990) posited that the exploration of how justice evaluations are made in the workplace provides a framework for organizations on how to guide future behaviors. Barsky et al. (2011) indicated that individuals' emotional reactions to fair treatment in organizational allocations and exchanges could have consequences at both perceptual and behavioral levels. Employees form judgments about fair and unfair treatment by comparing their situations regarding treatment and outcomes with those of others. Fairness in promotion affects perceptions of procedural justice and job satisfaction.

Cohen-Charash and Spector (2001) ascertained that perceptions of justice can be influenced by organizational practices, the organizational outcomes an individual receives, and the characteristics of the perceiver. Gill (2011) posited that when employees experience inequality, they develop a desire to prove their ability by increasing their output. Additionally, a key trust element is the expectation of one individual that another will treat them just or fairly, especially during the difficult times of strategic change. According to Bakhshi et al. (2009), Adams' theory advocated the determination of fairness through equity and conceptualized fairness by stating that employees determine whether they have been treated fairly or not by comparing their salaries with those of their colleagues who perform similar tasks. Organizational justice perceptions by non-managerial employees towards management are influenced by the development of close interpersonal relationships that are based on exchanges perceived as fair from the management. Finally, Rodell and Colquitt (2009) indicated that employees' perceptions of justice in their organizations are considered important for the well-being of employees as well as for effective organizational operations.

Research findings offer unique insights that organizational management should develop organizational justice towards employees because it affects workplace performance as a whole. Justice perceptions in the workplace have a direct impact on employees' attitudes and behaviors, and are considered important for the well-being of employees as well as for effective organizational operations. According to Williamson and Williams (2011), in this context, a manager's actions promoting fair treatment are more likely incorporated into the general fairness impression of employees in the workplace than would be the case in more stable times. Others scholars have indicated that perceptions of distrust and unfairness can lead to resistance to change and negative behaviors directed at organizations and management during change.

RESEARCH QUESTION #4

How can an organizational justice framework be used to explore employees' perceptions of the management of change within the context of strategic change?

Study findings indicate that a key way to gain employee trust, particularly in times of change, is to seek the opinions of employees and keep the promises made to them, in advance of any changes, particularly those that will have a direct impact on them. Findings indicate that this will help employees adjust to and accept any changes, rather than creating a resistance to change and adopting negative behaviors. Other findings indicate the importance of organizations to practice open and honest communication with employees to promote trust, even in the face of difficult change policy enactment. Without such open communication, employees are led to speculate negatively among themselves about management's motives and practices.

Saunders and Thornhill (2004) asserted that trust reduces uncertainty, in addition to complexity, as unfavorable expectations are removed and favorable expectations are seen as certain. Saunders (2011) ascertained that employees who feel trust can focus on positive aspects when talking about their reactions to organizational change. Managers should promote organizational justice and trust within the workplace environment and between employees, since scholars indicated that there is strong relationship between the two concepts, and that employees could be more efficient in order to increase organizational productivity. Research findings suggest interpersonal relationships between managers and non-managerial employees during periods of strategic changes can be strengthened through effective planning and effective decision-making and timely communication.

Research findings suggest that when management fulfills its obligations to employees in times of change organizational trust might increase. The study's findings indicate that in order to support change, both management and employees should visualize problems during a period of change in a real and tangible way in order to build trust and organizational commitment between them and support change. Other findings indicate that managers should communicate directly and openly to their employees, and empower employees during changes. Further study results indicate that employee trust in leadership could contribute to a successful change process, and leadership should consider increasing the participation of employees in the change process. Colquitt and Rodell (2011) ascertained that trust develops through an accumulation of experiences over time in the workplace. Salamon and Robinson (2008) and Zeidner (2008) suggested that management should employ practices in organizations to encourage trust because trust is a constructive and vital ingredient that promotes organizational effectiveness, and it is seen as a competitive advantage for organizations. Scholars have indicated that organizational trust is an important factor in order to reduce the complexity in organizational relationships. Other study findings indicate that management should clearly define responsibilities and roles along with clear and consistent policies and procedures during periods of strategic organizational change.

Chapter 9
Recommendations and Conclusions

Numerous researchers who studied the concepts of employees' perceptions of trust, fairness, and the management of change for more than 25 years, called for further studies to analyze employees' perceptional influences in organizational settings. Saunders and Thornhill (2003) recommended additional studies to examine employees' perceptions of trust, fairness, and the management of change, using an organizational justice framework in other sectors and in relation to different change situations. Saunders (2011) recommended further research to explore human resource management practices' impact upon both institutional trust reactions and the overall level of trust, in different organizational settings and in other sectors using an organizational justice framework. Other researchers called for studies to examine further justice research that could benefit from an alternative, contemporaneous, and complementary line of inquiry—one including overall justice judgments. Burnes and Jackson (2011) and Frazier et al. (2010) recommended further examination of employees' perceived organizational justice and how these can influence perceptions of trustworthiness for organizational leaders in other sectors. Elanain (2010) recommended the examination of the cultural norms and expectations people have that may explain the differential weighting of the different justice facets in shaping overall fairness across cultures. In response, this study provides further knowledge to help address these gaps in literature.

This multiple case study aimed to increase understanding of how an organizational justice perspective can be used as a framework to enhance our understanding of employees' perceptions of trust, fairness, and the management of change, and increase overall the successful implementation of strategic change within an organization. Results from this study suggest various contributions to the body of knowledge regarding helping organizational leadership recognize the significance of establishing mutual trust with their employees in order to successfully cooperate during times of strategic change. Indeed, study results indicate that employees' perceptions of trust may provide organizations with new insights regarding management's behavior during times of strategic changes in organizations. The present study will help organizational leadership better understand how to retain valuable employees, increase employees' perceptions of trust and fairness in the workplace, reduce employee turnover, and improve performance of the employees in an organization undergoing strategic change.

This study helped generate insights regarding factors that can help organizational management to consider fairness as an important element of trust and a critical element in any aspect of a change process. Results from this study suggest areas where management should focus in order to avoid unfairness and distrust in the workplace, which are considered to lead to negative as well as destructive responses towards the organization. Those who work in media organizations that are undergoing strategic changes may gain knowledge from reading the study findings, both management and subordinate employees. Managers might gain new insights for reading the results of this study, which could be used as guidelines to improve human resource management processes and procedures, including those relevant to change, the way they function, and formal and informal rules protecting employees' rights as well as organizational culture. Both managers and subordinates can increase their knowledge regarding organizational trust beyond individuals personally known to organizations or groups within them, helping them to create institutional trust for individuals at the organizational level.

Management might gain new insights from the results of this study that could be used in other media organizations or similar sectors to modify current approaches and formulate objectives to maximize their productivity, commitment and trust, and employees' motivation, job performance, teamwork spirit, and organizational relationships. Researchers who perform studies on trust, fairness, and the management of change using an organizational justice framework in organizations undergoing change may use the knowledge generated by this study to consider other types of research projects and for other sectors.

By reviewing study results, some researchers may generate ideas to perform longitudinal studies to examine the research area of trust, fairness, and the management of change using an organizational justice framework. Following, since organizational justice has been firmly linked with trust, fairness, commitment, citizenship behavior, customer satisfaction, and conflict resolution, it can guide organizations in all aspects when implementing strategic change in such a way that the change implementation process will be effective and successful. As a result, this study expands understanding of employees' perceptions of trust, fairness, and the management of change using an organizational justice framework for a media organization in Cyprus undergoing strategic change. This study represents a meaningful contribution to the understanding of organizational justice, trust, and the management of change in a specific media organization undergoing strategic change. Finally, media organizations may benefit from the study by understanding how employees' perceptions of trust, fairness, and the management of change can facilitate change sustainability in the future.

Recommendations

Although the findings of the study align with previous research and the literature, generalization of the findings or extrapolation for use in other settings cannot be done without caution. However, results from this study and the alignment with previous work and the theoretical literature support further recommendations for practical applications and future research opportunities. There are potential practical applications of the study findings and recommendations for further research that are presented in the subsequent paragraphs. Each potential application or recommendation for future research is made in alignment with research findings of the current study. Organizational leaders and managers who review the results of this study could be inspired to enhance an organization's efforts in accomplishing the desired results in times of change. Future studies could explore perceptions of trust, fairness, and the management of change in periods of strategic change in other sectors and in relation to different change situations. Research studies could examine management's perceptions of trust, fairness, and the management of change using an organizational justice framework in public and private sectors.

RECOMMENDATIONS FOR PRACTICE

Findings from this study suggest that management should build communications channels inside the organization between employees, in order to share information with employees. A recommended action for management is to build effective communication channels between the different departments in order to share information with employees on a continuous basis, so that trust can also be built. Another recommendation is that organizational leadership maintain open lines of communication vertically and horizontally, explain decisions, and utilize various forms of communication between employees. A further recommendation is to involve employees by allowing them to determine how their work is organized and carried out, and encourage decision-making and participation. Through continual communication people will feel more involved and connected to the process of change. Perceptions of trust and fairness could influence employees' reactions and attitudes towards a change initiative. Management should encourage employees to talk about their feelings and what they believe they will lose as a result of change, in order to establish mutual trust with the organization. Social relationships between employees and supervisors during change can build trust and is a critical factor for successful organizational changes. Closed communication channels between management and employees on issues of strategic change directly affecting employees' job security, salary, and benefits may generate employees' states of anger and resentment. To enhance open communication between managers and subordinates, management needs to understand that the process of informing employees and sharing information about the proposed change is an important factor in maintaining employee trust.

Other findings from this research indicate that employees want to feel their jobs will remain secure if they express views questioning the processes and tenets of strategic change within the organization. A recommended action for organizational management is to focus on promoting procedural justice in the workplace during times of change, which is seen as the perceived fairness of processes employed in the distribution of responsibilities, compensation, and rewards. A further recommendation is for organizations to develop a communication plan and assign roles and responsibilities to change management teams that will communicate on a frequent basis with employees. When managers employ procedural justice practices in the organization undergoing change, this may produce a positive impact on employee attitudes and can affect future performance and actions of employees. Further, greater loyalty and trust in the organization could be exhibited by employees if they perceive that a decision-making or change process is fair. Managers should be able to identify employees' perceptions of procedural justice because they are linked to their satisfaction with supervisors and commitment to the organization.

Results from this study suggest that for employees to generate fairness perceptions regarding organizational outcomes, the organization must allocate equality in their actions and decisions. A recommended action for management is to assess current allocation procedures in the workplace in order to be very attentive to employees' perceptions of fairness of proposed organizational outcomes, since employees seriously consider whether an outcome is fair or appropriate. When employees feel that there is distributive justice, they are more likely to feel more trusting towards management. On the other hand, when employees perceive unfair distribution of salaries, benefits, and responsibilities in the workplace they are more likely to present with low productivity, distrust, and low job dissatisfaction. Employees' justice perceptions can be moderated by events, such as strategic change, across an organization.

Results of this study further suggest that employees should be treated with dignity and respect during a period of strategic change in the organization and managers should focus on fair, honest, and truthful treatments towards employees. A recommended action for management is to focus more on interpersonal relationships in the workplace, an action enhancing employee performance and productivity. Another recommended action is to create a culture where relationships are important and demonstrate care and concern for employees' needs. The quality of interpersonal treatment is a critical determinant of an individual's assessment of justice, regardless of the outcome. A further recommended solution is for management to clearly define responsibilities and roles along with clear and consistent policies and procedures, so that employees are informed in a timely manner about any change or decision taking place in the organization undergoing change. A relationship exists between procedural justice and trust, with fairness perceptions of treatment (interactional justice) being very important in enabling trust in the workplace. Another recommended action for organizational management is to make fair decisions so that employees perceive their workplace as just and fair, enjoy job satisfaction, be less willing to leave the organization, and have a higher sense of commitment to their job. A further recommended action for management is to promote decisional judgments of honesty, ethical appropriateness, respect for rights and privacy, politeness, courtesy, keeping promises, and safeguarding secrets so employees' perceptions of fairness and trust remain high in times of change.

Research findings from this study indicate that management should promote communication and sharing of information in the workplace in order to build trust. A recommended action for management is to promote interpersonal trust that enhances creativity, empowerment, and teamwork during times of uncertainty and change, since during strategic change perceptions of outcomes may influence employee trust. Managers should employ mutually trusting relationships in the workplace with employees and, as a result, action and trust will reinforce each other. Other findings from this research suggest organizational management should understand how to assess a situation to determine the missing component in the trust process between management and supervisors and promote organizational relationships. A recommended action for management is to evaluate their actions towards their employees and promote trust when employees talk about organizational change. Employees' trust could reduce the complexity in organizational relationships during periods of change.

Other findings from this research indicate that employees are less willing to work in teams and their attitudes and behavior towards their peers change during organizational change. A recommended action for organizations is to promote organizational trust, which is at the core of all interpersonal relationships holding people together and offering individuals a sense of security. By promoting trust in the workplace, organizational management can offer many important benefits (derived from trust) for both organizations and employees. Further, employees who receive fair treatments from supervisors could have different perceptions about them. A further recommended action for managers is to assess current communication efforts with workers and evaluate influence on employees' perceptions of trust, fairness, and the management of change in the workplace. If communication is determined as transparent, employees will regard organizational change more favorably when, from their viewpoint, it has been fairly handled and elements of fairness (e.g., procedural, distributive, and interactional) in management's decision-making process can be easily observed.

RECOMMENDATIONS FOR FURTHER RESEARCH

Future studies could be performed to analyze how employee engagement, trust, and fairness are linked in organizations in other sectors undergoing strategic change using an organizational justice framework. Studies that examine the role of procedural fairness in trust and the management of change using an organizational justice framework in organizations undergoing change could also be performed.

Since this applied research study took place in Cyprus, national research studies could be performed to assess employees' perceptions of strategic change in media organizations located in areas such as Limassol and Paphos. The perceptions of participants who work in sales or who are technicians or cameramen from media organizations located in different geographical areas in Cyprus could be influenced by regional culture factors such as labor regulations, level of education, and literacy or gender.

Cross-national studies could be conducted to examine employees' perceptions of trust, fairness, and the management of change using an organizational justice framework in organizations undergoing change in other European countries and in other sectors. Participants who work in the media industry in job categories other than the ones included in this specific case study, such as television presenters, producers, journalists, or web producers, could have unique perceptions about trust, fairness, and the management of change in media organizations undergoing change that may differ from this study's participants. Further research studies could examine how managerial employees view organizational fairness and how this affects their behavior in the organization that is undergoing strategic change. Studies that focus on perceptions of participants who work in specific media departments, such as marketing, public relations, technology, and human resources, can be conducted to assess perceptions of how organizational trust, fairness, and the management of change influence departmental perceptions using an organizational justice framework.

Correlational studies could be performed to analyze relationships between employees' perceptions versus managements' perceptions of trust, fairness, and the management of change in an organizational context undergoing change using an organizational justice framework. For instance, individuals who work in sales, marketing, technical, or human resources departments could participate in studies to discuss perceptions about the ways that organizations should anticipate strategic changes and how this affects various organizational variables such as organizational commitment, employee engagement, counterproductive work behavior (i.e., employee theft), organizational performance, organizational citizenship behavior, and job performance.

Further research is needed to extend the current studies on trust, fairness, and the management of change in organizations undergoing change, measuring various aspects of trust in order to better understand the nature of organizational trust. For example, the behavioral intentions of trust could be a good measure of trust along with change behaviors as an outcome of trust. In this regard, we can extend the research that has focused only on the effect of trusting by other authors. Employees' positive perceptions of trust, the effect of being trusted by others, and the exercise of fair actions and decisions by organizational management is reported to improve individual performance and should be explored further in future research.

Future studies could be performed by researchers to examine employees' perceptions of trust, fairness, and the management of change using an organizational justice framework in organizations undergoing strategic change, in studies with more participants in order to explore further and test these relationships in different settings where change is not perceived as being implemented successfully or in other sectors. Additionally, studies that focus on the relationship between overall justice, specific types of justice, and employee attitudes and behavior in an organization undergoing strategic change could contribute to the organizational justice literature. Further research could examine the different dimensions of organizational justice present in each of the different types of justice in media organizations in Cyprus that are undergoing strategic changes, using an organizational justice framework.

Conclusions

A qualitative, multiple case study was conducted by one researcher to explore the perceptions of eight non-managerial participants who had at least three years of work experience in a media organization in Nicosia, Cyprus and who were active in sales, or carrying out responsibilities as technicians or cameramen, and had good and ample information on the issues under study. Of the eight participants, four worked in sales, two were technicians, and two worked as cameramen. This case study focused on employees' perceptions of trust, fairness, and the management of change in a privately-owned media organization in Cyprus that was undergoing a strategic change. During interview sessions, participants were asked seven semi-structured questions to solicit in-depth perceptions and opinions. Also, participants were asked to respond spontaneously with the first thoughts that came to their mind upon hearing four statements on psychological contract fulfillment based on an organizational justice framework. Semi-structured questions were used in this study to guide participants in expressing in-depth perceptions. Data saturation was achieved by the stated sample size. To validate participants' intended meanings, triangulation occurred in this study by corroborating results from hand-written field notes with content from transcriptions. Further triangulation occurred through member checking on the collected data.

Results indicate that participants did not identify discrepancies in interview transcriptions compared to interview responses. Frequently occurring words and emergent themes were identified and analyzed from transcriptions that were uploaded through NVivo software (Version 9) to compile, code, track, and analyze research data. Reliability was an important aspect of this research study, and lends credibility to findings and interpretations. Reliability was demonstrated in this study by minimizing errors with participant interviews, data collection, and recording. To help ensure reliability, the researcher used protocols and databases to capture relevant case study information. Having followed the approach of Yin (2009, 2012), the researcher used replication logic to show external validity, and as a result reliability was determined by the ability of the case study to be replicated in the future with similar findings. In addition, the researcher used multiple sources of evidence during data collection and explored the range of historical, attitudinal, and behavioral issues of the organization under study. This combination of approaches provided greater strength and validity of the research outcome.

This multiple case study aimed to enhance knowledge and reveal insights regarding employees' perceptions of trust, fairness, and the management of change using an organizational justice framework.

Organizational management and others can reference results of this multiple case study to enhance better understanding, and provide useful information to guide future research for organizations undergoing strategic changes. Key findings from this study, aligning with relevant research, suggest that organizational justice can act as an indicator for the effective implementation of a change initiative, be used as a contingency framework for understanding employees' perceptions of trust, fairness, and the management of change during strategic changes, and enable effective action in the organizational environment. Other important findings suggest that non-managerial employees build their judgments of organizations on elements of fairness that can be observed (e.g., distributive, procedural, and interactional), and all three organizational justice constructs are identified as moderators of employees' perceptions of fairness related to organizational change. Further findings indicate that organizations that are undergoing strategic change need to incorporate strategies and procedures that will facilitate successfully the change process. Research results further suggest that when management understands how the change in organizations can be successfully implemented, this would help them to forecast employee reactions and behaviors so as to bring about the desired change. Findings indicate that justice perceptions by non-managerial employees towards management in the specific organization under study are influenced by the development of close interpersonal relationships that are based on exchanges perceived as fair.

Further research results indicate fairness as an important trust element, where employees' perceptions of fairness can form key elements of individual perceptions of trust in an organization undergoing strategic change. Seminal researchers recommended additional studies to examine employees' perceptions of trust, fairness, and the management of change, using an organizational justice framework in other sectors and in relation to different change situations.

Other researchers recommended further examination of employees' perceived organizational justice and how this can influence perceptions of trustworthiness for organizational leaders in other sectors. Study results suggest various contributions to the body of knowledge regarding helping organizational leadership to recognize the significance of establishing mutual trust with their employees in order to successfully cooperate during times of strategic change. In addition, results from this study suggest how organizational leadership can better understand how to retain valuable employees, increase employees' perceptions of trust and fairness in the workplace, reduce employee turnover, and improve performance of the employees in an organization undergoing strategic change.

Future studies could be performed to examine the role of procedural fairness in trust and the management of change using an organizational justice framework in organizations undergoing change. Cross-cultural studies could also be conducted to examine employees' perceptions of trust, fairness, and the management of change using an organizational justice framework in organizations undergoing strategic change in other European countries and in other sectors. Following, future research studies could examine how managerial employees view organizational fairness and how this affects their behavior in the organization that is undergoing strategic change.

Bibliography

Ambrose, M., and Schminke, M. (2009). The role of overall justice judgments in organizational justice research: A test of mediation. *Journal of Applied Psychology, 94*(2), 491–500. doi:10.1037/a0013203

Bakhshi, A., Kumar, K., and Rani, E. (2009). Organizational justice perceptions as predictor of job satisfaction and organizational commitment. *International Journal of Business Management, 4*(9), 145–54. Retrieved from www.ccsenet.org/journal.html

Barsky, A., Kaplan, S., and Beal, D. (2011). Just feelings? The role of affect in the formation of organizational fairness judgments. *Journal of Management, 37*(1), 248–79. doi:10.1177/0149206310376325

Bartunek, J.M., and Rynes, S.L. (2010). Contributions of "Implications for Practice": What's in them and what might they offer? *Academy of Management Learning & Education, 9*(1), 100–117. Retrieved from http://amle.aom.org/content/9/1/100.full.pdf+html

Behson, S.J. (2011). Using relative weights to reanalyze 'settled' areas of organizational behavior research: The job characteristics model and organizational justice. *International Journal of Management & Information Systems, 14*(4), 43–55. doi:10.1177/0149206310364243

Bidarian, S., and Jafari, P. (2012). The relationship between organizational justice and trust. *Social and Behavioral Sciences, 47*, 1622–6. doi:10.1016/j.sbspro.2012.06.873

Bullock, R., and Batten, D. (1985). It's just a phase we're going through: A review and synthesis of OD phase analyses. *Group and Organization Studies, 10*, 383–412. doi:10.1177/105960118501000403

Burnes, B., and Jackson, P. (2011). Success and failure in organizational change: An exploration of the role of values. *Journal of Change Management, 11*(2), 133–62. doi:10.1080/14697017.2010.524655

Cohen-Charash, Y., and Spector, Y. (2001). The role of justice in organizations: A meta-analysis. *Journal of Applied Psychology, 86*(2), 278–321. Retrieved from http://www.ingentaconnect.com/content/els/07495978/2001/00000086/00000 002/art92958 [accessed 5 June 2013].

Colquitt, J.A. (2001). On the dimensionality of organizational justice: A construct validation of a measure. *Journal of Applied Psychology, 86*(3), 386–400.

Colquitt, J.A., Conlon, D.E., Wesson, M.J., Porter, C.O.L.H., and Ng, K.Y. (2001). Justice at the millennium: A meta-analytic review of 25 years of organizational justice research. *Journal of Applied Psychology, 86*, 425–45.

Colquitt, J.A., and Greenberg, J. (2003). Organizational justice: A fair assessment of the state of the literature. In J. Greenberg (ed.), *Organizational behavior: The state of the science* (pp. 165–210). Mahwah, NJ: Lawrence Erlbaum Associates.

Colquitt, J.A., and Rodell, J.B. (2011). Justice, trust, and trustworthiness: A longitudinal analysis integrating three theoretical perspectives. *Academy of Management Journal, 54*(6), 1183–206. Retrieved from http://dx.doi. org/10.5465/amj.2007.0572

Cropanzano, R., Byrne, S.Z., Bobocel, R.D., and Rupp, D.E. (2001). Moral virtues, fairness heuristics, social entities, and other denizens of organizational justice. *Journal of Vocational Behavior, 58*(2), 164–209. Retrieved from http:// leeds-faculty.colorado.edu/dahe7472/JVB%20-%202001a.pdf

Cummings, T., and Huse, E. (1989). *Organization development and change.* St. Paul, MN: West Publishing Company.

Dierendonck, D.V., and Jacobs, G. (2012). Survivors and victims, a meta-analytical review of fairness and organizational commitment after downsizing. *British Journal of Management, 23*, 96–109. doi:10.111/j.1467–8551.2010.0074.x

Eisenhardt, K.M., and Graebner, M.E. (2007). Theory building from cases: Opportunities and challenges. *Academy of Management Journal, 50*(1), 25–32. Retrieved from http://journals.aomonline.org/amj/editorials/Eisenhart. Graebner.2007.pdf

Elanain, H. (2010). Testing the direct and indirect relationship between organizational justice and work outcomes in a non-western context of UAE.

Journal of Management Development, 29(1), 5–27. doi:10.1108/02621711011009045

Folger, R., and Cropanzano, R. (1998). *Organizational Justice and Human Resource Management*. Beverly Hills, CA: Sage.

Frazier, M.L., Johnson, P.D., Gavin, M.J., Gooty, J., and Snow, B. (2010). Organizational justice, trustworthiness, and trust: A multifoci examination. *Group & Organization Management*, 35(1), 39–76. doi:10.1177/1059601109354801

Fulmer, A., and Gelfand, M. (2012). At what level (and in whom) we trust: Trust across multiple organizational levels. *Journal of Management*, 38(4), 1167–230. doi:10.1177/0149206312439327

Garcia-Izquierdo, A.L., Moscoso, S., and Ramos-Villagrasa, P.J. (2012). Reactions to the fairness of promotion methods: Procedural justice and job satisfaction. *International Journal of Selection and Assessment*, 20(4), 394–403. Retrieved from http://papers.ssrn.com/sol3/papers.cfm?abstract_id=2178863

Gill, R. (2011). Using storytelling to maintain employee loyalty during change. *International Journal of Business and Social Science*, 2(15), 23–32. Retrieved from http://www.ijbssnet.com/journals/Vol_2_No_15_August_2011/4.pdf

Gilstrap, J.B., and Collins, B.J. (2012). The importance of being trustworthy: Trust as a mediator of the relationship between leader behaviors and employee job satisfaction. *Journal of Leadership & Organizational Studies*, 19(2), 152–63. doi:10.1177/1548051811431827

Greenberg, J. (1987). A taxonomy of organizational justice theories. *The Academy of Management Review*, 12(1), 9–22. Retrieved from http://www.jstor.org/discover/10.2307/257990?uid=3737848&uid=2&uid=4&sid=21101470980893

Greenberg, J. (1990). Organizational justice: Yesterday, today, and tomorrow. *Journal of Management*, 16(2), 339–432. Retrieved from http://jom.sagepub.com/

Greenberg, J. (1993). The social side of fairness: Interpersonal and informal classes of organizational justice. In R. Cropanzano (ed.), *Justice in the Workplace: Approaching Fairness in Human Resource Management*. Hillsdale, NJ: Lawrence Erlbaum Associates, 79–103.

Greenberg, J. (2009). Everybody talks about organizational justice, but nobody does anything about it. *Industrial and Organizational Psychology*, *2*, 181–95. doi:1754–9426/09

Greenberg, J., and Baron, R. (2008). *Behavior in organizations* (9th ed.). Upper Saddle River, NJ: Pearson Education/Prentice Hall.

Groenewald, T. (2004). A phenomenological research design illustrated. *International Journal of Qualitative Methods*, *3*(1), 1–26. Retrieved from http://uir.unisa.ac.za/bitstream/handle/10500/2573/?sequence=1

Hausknecht, J.P., Sturman, M.C., and Roberson, Q.M. (2011). Justice as a dynamic construct: Effects of individual trajectories on distal work outcomes. *Journal of Applied Psychology*, *96*(4), 872–80. Retrieved from http://psycnet.apa.org/index.cfm?fa=buy.optionToBuy&id=2011–06122–001

Henderson, D.J., Wayne, S.J., Shore, L.M., Bommer, W.H., and Tetrick, L.E. (2008). Psychological Contract Fulfillment Scale [Database record]. Retrieved from PsycTESTS. doi:10.1037/t08712–000

Jones, D.A., and Skarlicki, D.P. (2012). How perceptions of fairness can change: A dynamic model of organizational justice. *Organizational Psychology Review*, *19*, 1–23. doi:10.1177/2041386612461665

Kim, T., Kim, G., and Kim, B. (2008). The effects of perceived justice on recovery satisfaction, trust, word-of-mouth, and revisit intention in upscale hotels. *Tourism Management*, *16*(3), 1–12. Retrieved from http://www.sciencedirect.com/science/article/pii/S0261517708000757

Lambert, E.G., Hogan, N.L., and Griffin, M.L. (2007). The impact of distributive and procedural justice on correctional staff job stress, job satisfaction, and organizational commitment. *Journal of Criminal Justice*, *35*, 644–56. Retrieved from http://www.phwa.org/resources/research/detail/1357

Lewin, K. (1951). *Field Theory in Social Science*. New York, NY: Harper and Row.

Lewin, K. (1958). Group decision and social change. In E.E. Maccoby, T.M. Newcomb, and E.L. Hartley (eds), *Readings in Social Psychology*. New York, NY: Henry Holt and Company, 197–211.

Lilly, J.D., Virick, M., and Hadani, M. (2010). The dynamic nature of justice: Influential effects of time and work outcomes on long-term perceptions of justice. *Social Justice Research*, 23(1), 37–59. doi:10.1007/s11211–010–0107–2

Lind, E.A., and van den Bos, K. (2002). When fairness works: Toward a general theory of uncertainty management. *Research in Organizational Behavior*, 24, 181–223. Retrieved from http://igitur-archive.library.uu.nl/fss/2006–0207–200108/bos_%202002_%20when_%20fairness_%20works_181.pdf [accessed 20 June 2013].

Mayer, D., Nishii, L., Schneider, B., and Goldstein, H. (2007). The precursors and products of justice climates: Group leader antecedents and employee attitudinal consequences. *Personnel Psychology*, 60(4), 929–63. doi:10.1111/j.1744–6570.2007.00096.x

Neves, P., and Caetano, A. (2006). Social exchange processes in organizational change: The roles of trust and control. *Journal of Change Management*, 6(4), 351–64. doi:10.1080=14697010601054008

Nonthaleerak, P., and Hendry, L. (2008). Exploring the six sigma phenomenon using multiple case study evidence. *International Journal of Operations & Production Management*, 28(3), 279–303. doi:10.1108/01443570810856198

Paille, P., and Dufour, M. (2012). Employee responses to psychological contract breach and violation: Intentions to leave the job, employer or profession. *The Journal of Applied Business Research*, 29(1), 205–16.

Patton, M.Q. (2002). *Qualitative Research & Evaluation Methods*. Thousand Oaks, CA: Sage Publications.

Rodell, J.B., and Colquitt, J.A. (2009). Looking ahead in times of uncertainty: The role of anticipatory justice in an organizational change context. *Journal of Applied Psychology*, 94(4), 989–1002. doi:10.1037/a0015351

Rousseau, D.M. (1995). *Psychological Contracts in Organizations*. London: Sage.

Rousseau, D.M., Sitkin, S.B., Burt, R.S., and Camerer, C. (1998). Not so different after all: A cross-discipline view of trust. *Academy of Management Review*, 23(2), 383–404. Retrieved from http://portal.psychology.uoguelph.ca/coursenotes/gill/7140/WEEK_3_Jan.25/Rousseau,%20Sitkin,%20Burt,%20%26%20Camerer_AMR1998.pdf

Rupp, D.E., and Cropanzano, R. (2002). The mediating effects of social exchange relationships in predicting workplace outcomes from multifoci organizational justice. *Organizational Behavior and Human Decision Processes*, *89*(1), 925–46. Retrieved from http://www.sciencedirect.com/science/article/pii/S0749597802000365

Saekoo, A. (2011). Examining the effect of trust, procedural justice, perceived organizational support, commitment, and job satisfaction in Royal Thai police: The empirical investigation in social exchange perspective. *Journal of Academy of Business and Economics*, *11*(3), 229–37. Retrieved from http://www.alacrastore.com/storecontent/Business-and-Management-Practices/272484651 [accessed 20 June 2013].

Salamon, S., and Robinson, S. (2008). Trust that blinds: The impact of collective felt trust on organizational performance. *Journal of Applied Psychology*, *93*(3), 593–601. doi:10.1037/0021–9010.93.3.593

Saunders, M. (2011). Trust and strategic change: An organizational justice perspective. In R. Searle and D. Skinner (eds), *Trust and Human Resource Management*. Cheltenham: Edward Elgar Publishing, 268–86.

Saunders, M., and Thornhill, A. (2003). Organizational justice, trust and the management of change: An exploration. *Personnel Review*, *32*(3), 360–75. doi:10.1108/00483480310467660

Saunders, M., and Thornhill, A. (2004). Trust and mistrust in organizations: An exploration using an organizational justice framework. *European Journal of Work and Organizational Psychology*, *13*(4), 493–515. doi:10.1080/13594320444000182

Saunders, M., and Thornhill, A. (2011). Researching sensitively without sensitizing: Using a card sort in a concurrent mixed methods design to research trust and distrust. *International Journal of Multiple Research Approaches*, *5*, 334–50. doi:10.5172/mra.2011.5.3.334

Six, F. (2007). Building interpersonal trust within organizations: A relational signaling perspective. *Journal Manage Governance*, *11*, 285–309. doi:10.1007/s10997–007–9030–9

Taylor, M.S. (2001). Reflections on fairness: Continuing the progression of justice research and practice. *Journal of Vocational Behavior*, *58*(2), 243–

53. Retrieved from http://www.ingentaconnect.com/content/ap/vb/2001/00 000058/00000002/art01796

Thornhill, A., and Saunders, M. (2003). Exploring employee's reactions to strategic change over time: The utilization of an organizational justice perspective. *Irish Journal of Management, 24*(1), 66–86. Retrieved from Business Source Complete database.

Tremblay, M., Cloutier, J., Simard, G., Chenevert, D., and Vandenberghe, C. (2010). The role of HRM practices, procedural justice, organizational support and trust in organizational commitment and in-role and extra-role performance. *The International Journal of Human Resource Management, 21*(3), 405–33. doi:10.1080/09585190903549056

van den Bos, K. (2001). Uncertainty management: The influence of uncertainty salience on reactions to perceived procedural fairness. *Journal of Personality and Social Psychology, 80*(6), 931–41. doi:10.1037/0022–3514.80.6.931

Weiss, H.M., and Cropanzano, R. (1996). Affective events theory: A theoretical discussion of the structure, causes and consequences of affective experiences at work. In B.M. Staw and L.L. Cummings (eds), *Research in Organizational Behavior: An Annual Series of Analytical Essays and Critical Reviews.* Greenwich, CT: JAI Press, 1–74.

Williamson, K., and Williams, K.J. (2011). Organizational justice, trust and perceptions of fairness in the implementation of agenda for change. *Radiography, 17*(1), 61–6. Retrieved from http://www.sciencedirect.com/ science/article/pii/S1078817410000878

Yin, R.K. (2009). *Case Study Research: Design and Methods* (4th ed.). Thousand Oaks, CA: Sage Publications.

Yin, R.K. (2012). *Applications of Case Study Research* (3rd ed.). Thousand Oaks, CA: Sage Publications.

Zeidner, R. (2008). Employees trust managers more than top brass. *Human Resources Magazine, 53*(10), 10. Retrieved from http://www.shrm.org/ Publications/hrmagazine/EditorialContent/Pages/1008execbrief.aspx

Index

For Product Safety Concerns and Information please contact our EU
representative GPSR@taylorandfrancis.com Taylor & Francis Verlag GmbH,
Kaufingerstraße 24, 80331 München, Germany

Printed and bound by CPI Group (UK) Ltd, Croydon, CR0 4YY
02/05/2025
01859284-0001